THE
High-Calcium
Low-Calorie
COOKBOOK

*250 Delicious Recipes to
Help You Beat Osteoporosis*

BY BETTY MARKS
with Hope Warshaw, M.M.Sc., R.D., C.D.E.

SURREY BOOKS

Chicago

For Alice

THE HIGH-CALCIUM LOW-CALORIE COOKBOOK is published by Surrey Books, Inc., 230 E. Ohio St., Suite 120, Chicago, IL 60611.

First edition: 1 2 3 4 5

This book is manufactured in the United States of America.

Library of Congress Cataloging-in-Publication Data
Marks, Betty.
   The high-calcium low-calorie cookbook : 250 delicious recipes to help you beat osteoporosis / Betty Marks.
    p. cm.
   ISBN 1-57284-059-5
   1. High-calcium diet—Recipes. 2. Low-calorie diet—Recipes.
3. Osteoporosis—Diet therapy—Recipes. I. Title.
   RM237.56 .M37 2003
   616.7'16—dc21

                                          2003012435

Editorial production: Bookcrafters, Inc., Chicago
Editorial Assistant: Anna Layton
Design and production: Joan Sommers Design, Chicago

For prices on quantity purchases or for a free book catalog, contact Surrey Books at www.surreybooks.com, or call 800-326-4430.

Distributed to the trade by Publishers Group West.

CONTENTS

FOREWORD   iv

PREFACE   vi

ACKNOWLEDGMENTS   viii

INTRODUCTION   ix

1   APPETIZERS   1
    Dips and Spreads   2
    Hors d'oeuvres   16

2   SOUPS   23

3   ENTREES   47
    Meat   48
    Poultry   53
    Seafood   60
    Pizza, Pasta, and Vegetable Pies   76
    Breakfast and Brunch Fare   91

4   VEGETABLES   103

5   GRAINS, NOODLES, AND POTATOES   127

6   SALADS   141

7   SALAD DRESSINGS   161

8   SAUCES   173

9   BREADS AND MUFFINS   181

10   DESSERTS   197
    Frozen Desserts   198
    Custards, Mousses, and Puddings   208
    Fruit Desserts   216
    Pies and Tarts   222

11   BEVERAGES   227
    Cold Drinks   228
    Hot Drinks   235

12   BASICS   237

APPENDIX: CALCIUM-RICH FOODS   257

INDEX   259

METRIC GUIDELINES   Inside Back Cover

FOREWORD

Osteoporosis has become a household word, but public understanding of this common and devastating disease has come slowly. For decades, medical scientists have known ways in which to prevent osteoporosis. But scientific knowledge does little without practical application, and people won't change if they don't understand, if they fear consequences of the changes, or if the change is too unpalatable. Betty Marks, in this splendid book, attacks the ignorance, the fear of side effects, and, most spectacularly, the unpalatability surrounding efforts to induce people to take an adequate amount of calcium in their diets.

While the word osteoporosis has become more familiar, misconceptions still abound. Osteoporosis means inadequate bone mass, which renders the afflicted person vulnerable to broken bones from trivial injury. Half of the women over 45 are so affected. Each year, over a million Americans break a bone because of osteoporosis, with resultant economic costs of billions of dollars.

Public familiarity with the complications of osteoporosis has improved because of advertising campaigns by calcium supplement manufacturers and the dairy industry. The ads have done the public a favor, but also may have contributed to some misunderstandings. Osteoporosis is not a calcium deficiency to be cured by taking large doses of calcium later in life. Osteoporosis is a complex disease with a combination of genetic and environmental influences, such as exercise, hormone balance, other medical problems, and diet.

In part, osteoporosis is a manifestation of poor health and dietary practices over a lifetime. A healthy diet, one that is not only rich in calcium but also adequate in other ways, is essential to bone health. It is essential during childhood, adolescence, and young adulthood when bones grow; it is essential through middle age when bones may be losing strength silently; and it is essential later in life when bones may break from minor injuries.

Every day, our bodies excrete calcium through urine, stool, and perspiration. We don't absorb all the calcium we take in. Old recommendations to ingest 800 mg per day are too low to cover losses and failure to absorb. But most American diets don't even contain that much. Everybody should get at least 1000 mg and postmenopausal women with susceptibility to osteoporosis should get 1500 mg, nursing mothers even more. When we lose more than we take in, our bones suffer.

Why have Americans damaged their bones by calcium deficient diets? One reason is they didn't know any better—that is no longer a valid reason. Another reason is that they thought a high-calcium diet meant a diet also high in cholesterol, fat, and calories. This cookbook invalidates that reason. Another reason is that they thought any diet that was medically prescribed as healthful meant tasteless and boring. This cookbook certainly refutes that.

One answer to calcium deficient diets is to take pills, which is certainly better than no answer. Most calcium pills are calcium carbonate-oyster shell calcium. But some people don't absorb calcium carbonate well, and some are constipated by it. Many people don't like to swallow pills, forget them, or have other reasons to avoid calcium supplements. For those people and for all who want to manage their health by simple, natural means, pills are not necessary. If there is adequate calcium in our diets, we don't need supplements.

Many people take pills because they think adequate dietary calcium means four big glasses of milk per day—too much fat, too much cholesterol, too many calories, and boring. Well, pills are boring too, but, as Betty Marks teaches us, pills aren't the only alternative. As you will read in this fun book, you can have a meal of Parmesan Sardine Appetizer, Oriental Snow Pea Soup, Coquilles St. Jacques with Green Beans Amandine, Middle East Cucumber Salad, a Parmesan Popover, and a glass of Mountain Valley (total calories 650), or you can swallow two 500 mg oyster shell pills. Both contain about the same amount of calcium. Which sounds best to you?

—David E. Fardon, M.D.
Past President, North American Spine Society

PREFACE

Mother was right to insist you drink your milk! The current interest in calcium backs her up, with milk cited as the best source of this vital mineral. Because of the high incidence of osteoporosis, women are particularly concerned with eating the proper foods to ward off this frightening brittle-bone disease. At the same time, care must be taken to control the high fat and calories contained in many milk products.

The National Institutes of Health have concluded that calcium and the female hormone estrogen are the mainstays of prevention and management of osteoporosis, which afflicts 34 million Americans aged 50 and older. A leading cause of bone fractures, osteoporosis can lead to other complications, causing permanent crippling and death.

Calcium does not regenerate itself, and so adequate quantities must be taken daily. In addition to contributing to strong bones, teeth, and muscles, calcium also fights high blood pressure, stress, colon cancer, and a host of other maladies. It is a natural tranquilizer and promotes blood clotting.

A well-balanced diet using low-fat milk products combined with daily sunshine and weight-bearing exercise, and perhaps a one-a-day vitamin supplement, will help maintain strong bones and overall good health. The earlier in life such a program is started, the better one can maintain continued good health.

Skim milk or nonfat dry milk, buttermilk, part-skim ricotta and low-fat cottage cheese, plain low-fat or nonfat yogurt, all help solve the dilemma of high fat. Delicious dishes can be made with the right combinations of these foods, as the following recipes show. Acidophilus milk, kefir, goat's milk, and soy milk are also low in fat and are good for people with lactose intolerance. Seaweeds, leafy green vegetables, dried figs, soy nuts, almonds, citrus fruits, sardines and salmon with their bones, oysters, tofu, and whole grains provide additional sources of good nourishment. Vitamins A, B complex, C, and D and the minerals iron, manganese, phosphorous, and potassium are also essential. All these nutrients are best taken from food rather than supplements, many of which have been proven harmful. The dishes in this cookbook are rich in minerals and vitamins.

I am a woman past menopause and I also have diabetes. Therefore, I am a prime candidate for osteoporosis. The meal plan I follow includes plenty of low-fat milk exchanges and other high-calcium foods. My earlier books, *Light & Easy Diabetes Cuisine* and *The Diabetes Double-Quick Cookbook*, contain many recipes with calcium, and from studying the nutritional needs of those with diabetes and brittle-bone disease, I have learned that everything is indeed connected. One hormone is dependent upon another, and just as the bones and connective tissues are interdependent, so are the vitamins and minerals we eat. What nourishes one helps nourish the other.

Drink your milk and eat your broccoli! Enjoy many marvelous meals from these recipes, and stay strong and healthy indefinitely!

    —Betty Marks
      New York City

ACKNOWLEDGMENTS

Without the help of Linda Fisher-Luther I could not have completed this book. Her imaginative and nutritious approach to cooking is reflected in the many recipes she contributed. I am grateful for her delicious dishes.

I am indebted to Dr. David E. Fardon for his Foreword and to Hope S. Warshaw, R. D., whose nutritional evaluation is critical to this book.

I am grateful to my friends who tasted and helped prepare many of the foods included in this volume.

The United Dairy Industry Association deserves my thanks, too, as does the Dairy Nutrition Council.

INTRODUCTION

Over the last several years we have all been bombarded with reports of deficient calcium consumption. We have also been well informed of the relationship between deficient calcium intake and the increase in bone fractures, especially in older women. Now the challenge is knowing how to increase calcium intake during the younger years to avoid the complications of insufficient calcium intake later in life. One may think that an easy cure-all is simply to take a calcium supplement. But as a nutritionist, I encourage individuals to obtain their calcium by making wise food choices. This is easier said than done. Statistically, women are most guilty of insufficient calcium intake. Many studies on calcium consumption show intakes that are often only half of the recommended dietary allowance (RDA). There are several researchers who believe that the RDA for calcium should be increased beyond 1,000 mg per day for adults.

Why has the consumption of calcium-rich foods decreased? High-calcium foods are often omitted because they are thought to be either unexciting, high in calories, or sometimes just plain inaccessible in our fast-paced world. Beyond good old fat-free or low-fat milk, the foods thought of as rich in calcium are usually ice cream, cheeses, cream sauces, puddings, etc. Not only are they all high in calcium but they are also high in fat, calories, and cholesterol.

The challenge that Betty Marks had in writing this cookbook was to find fun and creative ways in which to use the often overlooked low-calorie, high-calcium foods. Betty has met this challenge in several ways. Her recipes provide maximum calcium by incorporating low-fat, low-cholesterol alternatives, such as low-fat and evaporated skim milk, nonfat dry milk, low-fat cottage cheese and yogurt and other commonly available foods. Betty has also incorporated many of the lesser known high-calcium foods into tasty appetizers, entrees, desserts, and more. These include tofu, dried figs, dandelion greens, sardines, and salmon. Finally, Betty introduces us to new and unusual products, which increase the variety of foods from which we can choose.

The facts conclude that more calcium is needed in our daily diet. With this high-calcium, low-fat cookbook in hand, the opportunity is yours to make the task of consuming sufficient calcium enjoyable while at the same time building and maintaining strong bones and achieving optimal health.

—Hope S. Warshaw, M.M.Sc., R.D., C.D.E.
Nutrition Consultant
Alexandria, Virginia

CHAPTER 1 **APPETIZERS**

Any of these appetizers may be used as the first course of a meal or as an hor d'oeuvre or snack. Consult the nutrient information included with each recipe to determine which choices will fit in with your meals for the day. Try a dollop of Avocado Smoothie on a baked potato or serve Black Bean and Salmon Dip appetizer on a bed of lettuce for a luncheon main dish. Dare to be different and make your own delicious food combinations.

The dips may be served with raw vegetables such as string beans, carrot sticks, zucchini sticks, red or green bell pepper strips, radishes, and cauli-flower or broccoli florets or with low-fat whole wheat crackers, wasa bread, pita, tortillas, or toast. Celery, bok choy, and fennel are good for stuffing, too.

The inventive chef will want to try combinations of low-fat cottage cheese, ricotta, or yogurt with different vegetable purees and herbs. Sardines and salmon lend themselves to infinite variations when com-bined with fresh lemon or lime juice or mixed with high-calcium beans.

Many of the spreads may be thinned with a bit more milk or yogurt to make a succulent sauce or dressing. An extra sprinkle of parsley or grated cheese will add still more calcium.

AVOCADO SMOOTHIE

PER SERVING:
Calcium (mg): 26
Fat (g): 2
Chol (mg): .6
Carbo (g): 1.5
Protein (g): 2
Calories: 32

1 small avocado, peeled and pitted
(1 scant cup)
1 tablespoon fresh lemon juice
1 tablespoon nonfat dry milk
1 tablespoon minced scallion
1 cup low-fat cottage cheese
Salt and freshly ground black pepper
to taste
3 dashes cayenne pepper

Puree all ingredients in blender or food processor until smooth. Chill and serve with raw vegetables or whole wheat or rice crackers.

Makes 2 cups or 16, 2-tablespoon servings

BLACK BEAN AND SALMON DIP

8 corn tortillas

1 16-ounce can black beans, rinsed and drained

1 7-ounce can pink salmon with bones, drained

2 tablespoons safflower oil

1/4 cup fresh lime juice

1/4 cup chopped fresh Italian parsley

1/2 teaspoon onion powder

1/2 teaspoon celery salt

3/4 teaspoon ground cumin

3/4 teaspoon minced garlic

1/2 teaspoon grated lime zest

1/4 teaspoon dried red pepper flakes

1/4 teaspoon chili pepper

PER SERVING:
Calcium (mg): 36
Fat (g): 2
Chol (mg): 2
Carbo (g): 6.8
Protein (g): 3.6
Calories: 60

Cut tortillas into triangles and toast in 350°F oven until crisp. Mix together the drained beans and salmon, flaking the salmon with a fork. Mix in the oil and lime juice and all remaining ingredients except the tortillas. Chill to blend flavors. Serve with the tortilla chips. May also be used as an entree for 4, served on a bed of romaine lettuce.

Makes 2 1/2 cups or 20, 2-tablespoon servings

CAVIAR CHEESE DIP

PER SERVING:
Calcium (mg): 87
Fat (g): .3
Chol (mg): 1.2
Carbo (g): 2.6
Protein (g): 3.6
Calories: 56

3/4 cup part-skim ricotta cheese
1/4 cup low-fat cottage cheese
1 teaspoon fresh lemon juice
2 ounces red lumpfish caviar

Blend the cheeses with the lemon juice. Place in serving dish and top with caviar, or mix, as desired. Serve with rice crackers or whole wheat crisps or as an appetizer spread on baked potato skins or stuffed in celery. (It is also delicious as a topping for baked potatoes.)

Makes 1 cup or 8, 2-tablespoon servings

CHILI CON QUESO

PER SERVING:
Calcium (mg): 36
Fat (g): .3
Chol (mg): 1.2
Carbo (g): 2.6
Protein (g): 1
Calories: 17

1/2 cup orange-flavored Yogurt Sour Cream (see note below)
2 tablespoons chopped, seeded jalapeño pepper
1 clove garlic, minced
2 tablespoons minced onion or scallion

Stir together all ingredients. Serve with crudités or toasted tortilla chips.

Note: To make orange-flavored Yogurt Sour Cream, follow the recipe for Yogurt Sour Cream (see pg. 254), using 1 cup plain non-fat yogurt and 2 tablespoons concentrated frozen orange juice.

Makes 3/4 cup or 12, 1-tablespoon servings

CLAM CHEESE DIP

1/2 cup chopped clams
1/4 cup low-fat cottage cheese
3/4 cup part-skim ricotta cheese
1/4 cup chopped onion
1 clove garlic, sliced
1/2 teaspoon celery salt
1 teaspoon drained capers
1 teaspoon fresh lemon juice
1 teaspoon anchovy paste
1/4 teaspoon dried thyme
    Dash white pepper
    Dash cayenne pepper
    Paprika
    Sprig parsley

PER SERVING:
Calcium (mg): 80
Fat (g): 2.2
Chol (mg): 6.5
Carbo (g): 2.1
Protein (g): 5.6
Calories: 52

Combine all ingredients except paprika and parsley in blender or food processor. Garnish with dusting of paprika and place parsley sprig in center. Serve with vegetable crudités or crackers.

Makes 1 cup or 8, 2-tablespoon servings

CONFETTI VEGETABLE DIP

PER SERVING:
Calcium (mg): 69
Fat (g): 1.5
Chol (mg): 6
Carbo (g): 2.5
Protein (g): 2.5
Calories: 34

1 cup part-skim ricotta cheese

½ cup plain low-fat yogurt

½ cup shredded carrot

¼ cup sliced scallion

2 tablespoons chopped red bell pepper

2 tablespoons chopped green bell pepper

2 tablespoons finely chopped celery

¼ teaspoon salt

⅛ teaspoon freshly ground black pepper

Mix ricotta and yogurt until smooth. Add remaining ingredients. Cover and refrigerate to combine flavors until ready to serve. Serve with additional fresh vegetables, whole wheat crackers, or pita bread triangles.

Makes about 1¾ cups or 14, 2-tablespoon servings

FANCY FENNEL DIP

1 cup low-fat cottage cheese

½ cup grated sharp Cheddar or Colby cheese

2 tablespoons buttermilk

1 tablespoon nonfat dry milk

1 teaspoon fennel or dill seeds

¼ teaspoon dry mustard

⅛ teaspoon freshly ground black pepper

Pinch cayenne pepper

1 tablespoon chopped scallions

Paprika

Minced fresh parsley

PER SERVING:
Calcium (mg): 40
Fat (g): 13
Chol (mg): 4.5
Carbo (g): .8
Protein (g): 2.8
Calories: 27

Blend all ingredients except paprika and parsley in food processor and chill. Garnish with a little paprika and minced parsley.

Makes 2 cups or 16, 2-tablespoon servings

VEGETABLE GUACAMOLE

PER SERVING
(includes one tortilla):
Calcium (mg): 21
Fat (g): 2.9
Chol (mg): .1
Carbo (g): 13.8
Protein (g): 3.6
Calories: 109

$\frac{1}{2}$ cup peeled, pitted, and sliced avocado

1 tablespoon fresh lime juice

$\frac{1}{2}$ cup fresh peas

$\frac{1}{2}$ cup broccoli florets

$\frac{1}{4}$ cup peeled, chopped, and seeded ripe tomatoes

$\frac{1}{4}$ cup chopped fresh coriander leaves (cilantro)

1 clove garlic, minced

1 small green chili, seeded and sliced

2 tablespoons nonfat dry milk

2 tablespoons chopped onion

10 corn tortillas

Using a fork, mash avocado slices with lime juice. Blanch peas and broccoli (any other green vegetable may be used) and puree. Mix with avocado and add remaining ingredients except the tortillas. Cut these into wedges and spread on cookie sheet to bake until crisp in 350°F oven. Serve wedges with the dip.

Makes about 2 cups or 10, 3-tablespoon servings

HEAVENLY HUMMUS

2 cups cooked garbanzo beans (chickpeas), if canned, rinse and drain

2 tablespoons buttermilk

$1/4$ cup toasted sesame seeds

3 tablespoons fresh lemon juice

1 teaspoon sesame oil

1 tablespoon low-sodium soy sauce

2 cloves garlic, sliced

1 teaspoon ground cumin

Pinch freshly ground black pepper

3 dashes cayenne pepper

PER SERVING:
Calcium (mg): 29
Fat (g): 2.6
Chol (mg): .3
Carbo (g): 11.7
Protein (g): 5
Calories: 85

Mix all ingredients in food processor until well blended. Add more buttermilk to adjust consistency. Serve with raw vegetables, whole wheat crackers, or pita bread.

Makes 1 cup or 8, 2-tablespoon servings

LIPTAUER CHEESE

PER SERVING:
Calcium (mg): 55
Fat (g): 2.6
Chol (mg): 5
Carbo (g): 1.5
Protein (g): 2.2
Calories: 40

$1/2$ cup part-skim ricotta cheese

2 tablespoons nonfat dry milk

1 tablespoon safflower oil

1 teaspoon drained capers

1 teaspoon Hungarian sweet paprika

$1/2$ teaspoon anchovy paste

1 tablespoon caraway seeds

1 tablespoon chopped scallion

Salt and freshly ground pepper to taste

Mix all ingredients together and refrigerate for about 8 hours. Serve with whole wheat or rice crackers or rye bread.

Makes 1 cup or 8, 2-tablespoon servings

MISO MANIA

1 cup tofu (bean curd), cut into chunks

3 tablespoons miso (fermented barley or soy paste, see pg. 241)

¼ cup water

1 teaspoon sesame oil

1 tablespoon fresh lemon juice

¼ teaspoon crushed red pepper flakes

2 scallions, chopped

2 tablespoons crunchy peanut butter

3 tablespoons plain low-fat yogurt

Alfalfa sprouts

PER SERVING:
Calcium (mg): 28
Fat (g): 1.9
Chol (mg): .2
Carbo (g): 1.2
Protein (g): 1.9
Calories: 23

Mix all ingredients except alfalfa sprouts in food processor or blender until smooth. Serve on warm pita bread triangles with alfalfa sprout topping or over fresh garden vegetables.

Makes 2 cups or 16, 2-tablespoon servings

PARMESAN SARDINE APPETIZER

PER SERVING:
Calcium (mg): 124
Fat (g): 3.1
Chol (mg): 23.7
Carbo (g): 1.9
Protein (g): 5
Calories: 49

1 3¾-ounce can water-packed sardines with bones

2 tablespoons plain low-fat yogurt

2 tablespoons grated Parmesan or sapsago cheese

1 tablespoon chopped scallion

1 teaspoon Dijon mustard

1 teaspoon grated lemon zest

3 teaspoons fresh lime or lemon juice
    Freshly ground black pepper to taste
    Dash cayenne pepper

1 teaspoon toasted sesame seeds

4 romaine lettuce or spinach leaves

Drain sardines and mash with a fork. Stir in yogurt, cheese, and all remaining ingredients except sesame seeds and lettuce. Place in small serving bowl. Top with sprinkling of sesame seeds and chill a few hours. Make individual servings on beds of romaine lettuce or spinach leaves as first course or serve as hors d'oeuvres on Japanese rice crackers.

Makes 4 first-course servings

PICKLE PEPPER SPREAD

1/4 cup low-fat cottage cheese
3/4 cup part-skim ricotta cheese
1/4 cup grated sharp Cheddar cheese
1 teaspoon Dijon mustard
2 tablespoons chopped dill pickles
2 tablespoons chopped pimiento
2 tablespoons chopped green pepper

PER SERVING:
Calcium (mg): 71
Fat (g): 2.5
Chol (mg): 9
Carbo (g): 1.1
Protein (g): 3.3
Calories: 40

Combine all ingredients in food processor, saving some of the pimiento and green pepper for garnish when serving. Chill and serve as spread on rice crackers or toast.

Makes about 1 1/2–2 cups or 12–16, 2-tablespoon servings

SIMON'S SIMPLE SALMON DIP

1 cup low-fat cottage cheese
5 ounces canned pink salmon with bones
1 tablespoon minced scallion or chives
2 tablespoons plain low-fat yogurt or buttermilk
1 teaspoon fresh lemon juice
2 tablespoons diced dill pickles
  Dash Tabasco
  Salt and freshly ground pepper to taste
  Parsley for garnish

PER SERVING:
Calcium (mg): 32
Fat (g): .7
Chol (mg): 4
Carbo (g): .9
Protein (g): 3.6
Calories: 25

Combine all ingredients except parsley in blender or food processor. Adjust seasoning. Garnish with parsley. Serve with rice crackers, whole wheat crackers, toast, or fresh vegetables.

Makes 2 cups or 16, 2-tablespoon servings

SUZANNE'S SPINACH APPETIZER

PER SERVING:
Calcium (mg): 88
Fat (g): 3.7
Chol (mg): 0
Carbo (g): 3.3
Protein (g): 3.8
Calories: 56

10 ounces fresh spinach, washed and trimmed
12 ounces firm tofu (bean curd), cut into chunks
 3 tablespoons fresh lime or lemon juice
 2 tablespoons safflower oil
 2 cloves garlic, minced
 1 teaspoon dried oregano, crushed
 1/4 teaspoon salt
    Dash freshly grated nutmeg
    Freshly ground black pepper to taste
    Extra spinach leaves
 1 red bell pepper, sliced into julienne strips

Place all ingredients except extra spinach leaves and bell pepper strips in a food processor and blend together. Place in refrigerator to combine flavors. When ready to serve, place on bed of spinach leaves and surround with bell pepper strips or place strips in a small cup in center of dip. Nice with other fresh garden vegetables, too.

Makes about 3 cups or 12, 1/4-cup servings

TOMATO DIP

½ cup plain low-fat yogurt

¾ cup low-fat cottage cheese, rinsed and drained

¼ cup tomato or V-8 juice

1 tablespoon dried onion flakes

¼ teaspoon dry mustard

1 teaspoon fresh lime juice

2 tablespoons tomato paste

1 teaspoon chopped dill pickles

1 teaspoon low-sodium soy sauce

1 teaspoon chopped fresh parsley

PER SERVING:
Calcium (mg): 20
Fat (g): .6
Chol (mg): 1
Carbo (g): 1.5
Protein (g): 1.8
Calories: 19

Fold the yogurt into the drained cottage cheese and then blend in remaining ingredients, sprinkling the parsley on top as garnish. Serve with crudités, whole wheat crackers, or bread or use as sauce for cooked fish or vegetables.

Makes 2 cups or 16, 2-tablespoon servings

TRICOLOR YOGURT LOAF

PER SERVING:
Calcium (mg): 274
Fat (g): 9.9
Chol (mg): 12
Carbo (g): 12
Protein (g): 8.9
Calories: 170

4 cups plain Yogurt Sour Cream
(see note below)

1 envelope unflavored gelatin

¼ cup cold water

1 tablespoon crystalline fructose

1½ cup Crème Fraîche (see pg. 250)

1 teaspoon salt

3 tablespoons walnut oil

Dash white pepper

⅓ cup sliced scallions, including green parts

2 tablespoons minced fresh parsley

⅓ cup peeled, seeded, and chopped tomatoes

About 1 cup romaine lettuce or
spinach greens

3 tablespoons chopped toasted almonds

When yogurt has drained, transfer to a large mixing bowl. In a cup, soften gelatin in cold water. In a small saucepan, mix the gelatin, fructose, Crème Fraîche, and salt. Stir over gentle heat until gelatin dissolves. Turn into the yogurt along with walnut oil and pepper. Stir to blend.

In the meantime, line a 5-inch by 8-inch loaf pan with plastic wrap, extending it over the sides of the pan. Then pour one-third of the yogurt mixture into the loaf pan.

Combine scallions with parsley and sprinkle one-third of the mixture over the yogurt in pan. Cover with half of remaining yogurt. Spread over this half of the chopped tomatoes. Over this layer spread rest of the yogurt. Fold the plastic wrap over the top and refrigerate for about 4 hours.

When ready to serve, or a few hours ahead of time, invert loaf pan onto lettuce-lined serving plate. Garnish the top of the yogurt loaf with three alternating bands of the remaining scallions and parsley mixture, remaining chopped tomatoes, and almonds. Serve with crisp crackers as an appetizer or a luncheon dish. Will keep well refrigerated up to 2 days.

Note: To make 4 cups plain Yogurt Sour Cream, follow the recipe for Yogurt Sour Cream (see pg. 254), using 8 cups plain low-fat yogurt.

Serves 8

CORNY TOFU STICKS

PER SERVING:
Calcium (mg): 102
Fat (g): 4.8
Chol (mg): 24
Carbo (g): 18.6
Protein (g): 6.7
Calories: 142

Vegetable spray

1 pound firm tofu (bean curd)

1 cup nonfat dry milk

2 eggs (1 yolk only)

2 tablespoons vegetable oil

1 tablespoon crystalline fructose

1/2 cup buttermilk

1/4 cup whole wheat flour

1 1/2 teaspoons baking powder

1 1/2 cups cornmeal

Preheat oven to 425°F. Coat 2 cornstick pans (6 sticks each) or one 8-inch square pan with vegetable oil spray. In a blender or food processor, mix the tofu, nonfat dry milk, eggs, oil, fructose, and buttermilk. Process until smooth.

Mix the dry ingredients together, then combine with tofu mixture. Stir to mix gently. Bake the sticks for 20 minutes or the square pan for 25–30 minutes until the top is brown and springs back when touched lightly.

Makes 12 sticks (1 per serving) or 16, 2-inch squares

OYSTERS ON THE HALF SHELL

1 dozen fresh bluepoint or other oysters
Lemon wedges
Grated horseradish

PER SERVING:
Calcium (mg): 84
Fat (g): 1.8
Chol (mg): 48
Carbo (g): 3
Protein (g): 7.8
Calories: 60

Purchase oysters from a reliable fish market, making certain they are alive and fresh. Keep refrigerated until ready to serve. Shuck (see pg. 244), and serve on the half shell on a bed of ice with lemon wedges, horseradish, or any other sauce desired.

Makes 2, 6-oyster servings

SARDINE SQUASH

4 cups raw acorn or butternut squash (cooks down to 2 cups)

1 tablespoon vegetable oil

½ cup chopped onion

1 clove garlic, minced

¼ cup Chicken Stock (see pg. 247)

4 tablespoons fresh lime or lemon juice

2 teaspoons grated lemon zest

1 teaspoon dried dill weed

Salt and freshly ground pepper to taste

1 7½-ounce can sardines with bones, in tomato sauce

Lemon slices

Parsley sprigs

4 romaine lettuce or spinach leaves (optional)

Peel and seed the squash and grate to make 4 cups. Heat the oil in a large nonstick skillet with onion and garlic. Add squash, broth, lime or lemon juice, zest, and dill. Cover and steam for 3 minutes. Add salt and pepper, then remove from heat and turn out onto plates. Arrange the sardines and tomato sauce over the squash and garnish with lemon slices and parsley sprigs. Place on lettuce or spinach leaves, if desired.

Serves 4 as an appetizer

SARDINE-STUFFED MUSHROOMS

12 medium-sized mushroom caps (stems removed), wiped clean

1 3¾-ounce can water-packed sardines including bones, drained

¼ teaspoon dried dill weed

2 teaspoons Dijon mustard

1 tablespoon fresh lime juice

12 capers, drained and chopped

Parsley sprigs or fresh chopped parsley

Paprika

PER SERVING:
Calcium (mg): 23
Fat (g): .6
Chol (mg): 7
Carbo (g): .6
Protein (g): 1.6
Calories: 14

Mash sardines with the dill, mustard, lime juice, and capers. Stuff into the mushroom caps. Garnish with parsley and a dash of paprika.

Serves 12

STUFFED GRAPE LEAVES

PER SERVING:
Calcium (mg): 30
Fat (g): 2.2
Chol (mg): 0
Carbo (g): 5.5
Protein (g): 1.2
Calories: 44

2 tablespoons vegetable oil, divided

¾ cup minced onion

⅓ cup brown rice

1¼ cups water

1 tablespoon sunflower seeds

1 tablespoon minced fresh parsley

1 tablespoon chopped fresh mint or
   1 teaspoon dried

Freshly ground pepper to taste

1 tablespoon raisins

15 grape leaves

2 tablespoons cold water

Lemon wedges

In a nonstick skillet, heat 1 tablespoon of vegetable oil and sauté onion. Add uncooked rice and stir until grains are coated. Add 1¼ cups water and bring to simmer. Cover pan and cook until rice is tender and all water absorbed, about 20 to 30 minutes. Add more water if necessary. Lightly brown sunflower seeds in another skillet and add to cooked rice with parsley, mint, pepper, and raisins.

In the meantime, blanch grape leaves in boiling water and separate. Place on paper toweling, dull sides up. Stuff each leaf with rice mixture to form small bundles. Stack stuffed leaves seam side down in a large casserole. Add 2 tablespoons cold water and sprinkle with remaining tablespoon of oil. Cover and simmer 30 minutes. Serve at room temperature with lemon wedges.

Serves 15

CHAPTER 2 **SOUPS**

Soup may begin a meal or may be the main course, served with a bright green salad and good hearty bread, muffins, or crisp crackers. Soup may be thin, such as Oriental Snow Pea Soup, or thick, such as Mexican Corn Chowder and Connie's Iowa Bean Soup. The creamy Salmon Bisque is rich and delicious and provides a big calcium kick.

For the cream soups, buttermilk, yogurt, and skim milk are all interchangeable, according to your taste. Remember, yogurt should not be boiled! When making soups that call for it, just heat quickly at the end of the preparation and serve warm. Add nonfat dry milk to any soup for still more calcium.

Vegetables other than those specified may be substituted—celery or mushrooms instead of carrots, broccoli in place of zucchini, fish instead of shrimp, lobster rather than fish. Most will work well with a simple adjustment of spices and seasonings.

Colorful garnishes sprinkled on soup can give extra calcium and appeal. Try a teaspoon of chopped parsley or basil, red and green bell peppers chopped fine, some thinly shredded carrots, or a sprinkling of paprika or nutmeg.

In a pinch, if you're caught short of a specified stock, use Vogue Instant Chicken or Vegetable Flavored Base, available in most health food stores and supermarkets.

Note: The blender or food processor is indispensable in making pureed soups, but never pour hot liquid directly into it. Let the soup cool, then add a little at a time and return to saucepan when mixed.

ASPARAGUS POTAGE

PER SERVING:
Calcium (mg): 172
Fat (g): 2.7
Chol (mg): 8
Carbo (g): 16.6
Protein (g): 7.2
Calories: 116

$\frac{1}{2}$ cup cooked potato, cut into chunks

$\frac{1}{2}$ cup chopped onion

2 cups Vegetable Stock or Chicken Stock (see pg. 247)

2 cups fresh asparagus, trimmed and cut into 2-inch pieces

$\frac{1}{4}$ cup chopped carrot

2 tablespoons whole wheat flour

Freshly ground black pepper

2 tablespoons dry sherry or vermouth

$\frac{1}{2}$ teaspoon salt

Dash cayenne pepper

$\frac{1}{2}$ teaspoon grated lemon zest

Dash dried thyme

Dash dried mint

2 cups buttermilk

Fresh chopped parsley or chives

Cook potato and onion in the stock for about 10 minutes. Add remaining ingredients except buttermilk and parsley or chives. Bring to boil and cook until asparagus is tender, about 5 minutes. Remove from heat, let cool, and—a little at a time—puree in blender or food processor. Return to saucepan and stir in buttermilk. Garnish with chopped parsley or chives. Serve warm or chilled.

Makes about 4$\frac{1}{2}$ cups or 4, 1$\frac{1}{8}$-cup servings

BUTTERMILK BROCCOLI SOUP

1 teaspoon vegetable oil

½ cup chopped onion

1 clove garlic, minced

3 cups cut-up broccoli florets and stems

2 cups buttermilk

1 teaspoon cumin seed

Pinch freshly grated nutmeg

1 tablespoon chopped fresh parsley

1 tablespoon diced red bell pepper

PER SERVING:
Calcium (mg): 242
Fat (g): 3
Chol (mg): 5
Carbo (g): 18.4
Protein (g): 11.2
Calories: 129

In nonstick skillet, heat the oil and sauté onion and garlic. Add broccoli to pan and toss for 1 minute. Turn into food processor with remaining ingredients, except parsley and peppers, and blend until smooth. Serve with garnish of parsley and peppers.

Makes about 6 cups or 4, 1½-cup servings

CARIOCA BEAN SOUP

2 cups dried black beans

3 cups Vegetable Stock or Beef Stock (see pgs. 247, 246)

1 large onion, chopped

2 stalks celery, chopped

1 bay leaf

7 cups water

$\frac{1}{4}$ teaspoon salt

Dash freshly ground black pepper

1 teaspoon chopped jalapeño pepper or $\frac{1}{2}$ teaspoon crushed dried red pepper

2 tablespoons dry sherry

10 slices lemon

Chopped parsley

Cover beans with salted water by two inches and let soak overnight, draining periodically and replacing water. When ready to prepare soup, drain again. Place the drained beans in a large kettle with all the ingredients except sherry, lemon, and parsley. Cover and bring to boil. Skim off any froth that accumulates, and simmer covered over low heat for about 3 hours or until beans and vegetables are tender. Remove soup from pot, let cool, and little by little puree in blender or food processor. Adjust seasoning, add sherry, and return to kettle to warm. Serve soup topped with lemon slice and sprinkling of parsley.

Makes 10 cups or 10, 1-cup servings

CHILLY CANNELLINI SOUP

1 15-ounce can cannellini beans (white kidney beans), drained and rinsed

½ cup plain low-fat yogurt

¾ cup skim milk

1 clove garlic, chopped

1 small onion, chopped

1 tablespoon finely chopped fresh basil or 1 teaspoon dried

Salt and freshly ground black pepper to taste

Dash cayenne pepper

Extra yogurt

1 tablespoon chopped fresh parsley

PER SERVING:
Calcium (mg): 148
Fat (g): 1
Chol (mg): 3
Carbo (g): 24.5
Protein (g): 9.8
Calories: 143

Place all ingredients except extra yogurt and parsley in food processor or blender and puree until smooth. Pour into a bowl and chill 2–3 hours before serving. Serve with dollop of yogurt and sprinkling of parsley.

Makes about 2 cups or 4, ½-cup servings

COTTAGE CHEESE SOUP

1 tablespoon Best Butter (see pg. 249)

1 small onion, chopped fine

1 stalk celery, chopped

1 green bell pepper, cored, seeded, and chopped fine

1/2 teaspoon salt

1/4 teaspoon freshly ground black pepper

1/4 teaspoon Hungarian sweet paprika

1 cup water

2 cups skim milk

1/2 cup low-fat cottage cheese

2 tablespoons part-skim ricotta cheese

Heat the Best Butter in a nonstick skillet and cook the onion, celery, and green peppers 5 minutes or until tender. Add the salt, pepper, paprika, water, and milk. Cover and cook over low heat about 15 minutes. Just before serving, add the cottage cheese and ricotta, stirring to blend. Do not let boil.

Makes 4 cups or 4, 1-cup servings

CREAM OF MUSHROOM SOUP

1 teaspoon Best Butter (see pg. 249)

¼ cup minced onion

⅓ cup chopped celery

2 cups thinly sliced fresh mushrooms

2 cups skim milk

2 tablespoons nonfat dry milk

1½ tablespoons whole wheat flour or cream of wheat

½ teaspoon salt

Dash freshly ground black pepper

Dash cayenne pepper

Dash freshly grated nutmeg

2 tablespoons dry sherry

Paprika

1 tablespoon chopped fresh parsley

PER SERVING:
Calcium (mg): 192
Fat (g): 1.5
Chol (mg): 4
Carbo (g): 14.2
Protein (g): 7
Calories: 96

Heat Best Butter in a nonstick saucepan and sauté onions and celery; add mushroom slices and cook until tender. Mix remaining ingredients except paprika and parsley in blender or food processor; then add the mushroom mixture and blend again. Pour back into the saucepan and heat gently until soup thickens, stirring. Garnish with paprika and parsley to serve.

Makes 4 cups or 4, 1-cup servings

CREAMY CARROT SOUP

PER SERVING:
Calcium (mg): 151
Fat (g): 3.5
Chol (mg): 6
Carbo (g): 20
Protein (g): 3.6
Calories: 108

2 teaspoons Best Butter (see pg. 249)

1 teaspoon whole wheat flour

2 cups scraped and sliced carrots

2 cups Vegetable Stock (see pg. 247)

Pinch salt

1 sprig fresh thyme or ¼ teaspoon dried, crumbled

1 bay leaf

½ teaspoon fresh ginger (optional)

1 teaspoon concentrated frozen orange juice

Freshly ground pepper

1 cup skim milk

2 tablespoons nonfat dry milk

Few sprigs fresh mint or ½ teaspoon dried mint or fresh chopped parsley

In nonstick saucepan, heat Best Butter and stir in whole wheat flour. Add carrots, Vegetable Stock, and salt and bring to boil. Add thyme, bay leaf, and ginger, if desired. Reduce heat and simmer until tender, about 8 minutes.

With slotted spoon, remove ¼ cup of carrots and reserve for garnish. Skim off any froth that accumulates. Let cool, remove bay leaf, and pour into food processor, a little at a time, to blend.

Return to saucepan, add orange juice concentrate, pepper to taste, and milk. Heat through, stirring. Serve with garnish of fresh mint or parsley and reserved carrots. May also be served cold.

Makes 4 cups or 4, 1-cup servings

CUCUMBER BUTTERMILK SOUP

2 cups peeled, seeded, and chopped cucumbers

4 cups buttermilk

1 tablespoon fresh lemon juice

2 tablespoons chopped scallion

1 tablespoon chopped fresh mint or 1 teaspoon dried

1 tablespoon chopped fresh dill or 1 teaspoon dried

1 teaspoon ground cumin seed

Dash white pepper

1 tablespoon fresh chopped parsley

PER SERVING:
Calcium (mg): 297
Fat (g): 2.2
Chol (mg): 9
Carbo (g): 13.4
Protein (g): 8.3
Calories: 109

Place all ingredients except parsley in blender or food processor and blend until smooth. Garnish with fresh parsley. Serve cold.

Makes 5 cups or 4, 1¼-cup servings

KALE SOUP

PER SERVING:
Calcium (mg): 114
Fat (g): 2.3
Chol (mg): 1
Carbo (g): 19.3
Protein (g): 5.7
Calories: 114

½ pound fresh kale, well washed

4 cups Chicken Stock (see pg. 247)

Pinch salt

¼ teaspoon freshly ground black pepper

3 medium potatoes, peeled and sliced thin

1 teaspoon safflower oil

2 cloves garlic, minced

6 slices lemon

Dash cayenne pepper

Discard tough stems and any discolored kale leaves. Shred or chop kale very fine. Place all ingredients except lemon and cayenne in a saucepan and cook until potatoes are tender. Remove potatoes and mash, then return to the broth and bring to a boil. Serve with lemon slices and dash of cayenne.

Makes 6 cups or 6, 1-cup servings

LOBSTER AND TOMATO BISQUE

1 lobster, 1½–2 pounds

2 cups canned Italian plum tomatoes

¼ cup finely chopped onion

1 bay leaf

2 large fresh leaves basil, chopped, or
½ teaspoon dried basil

2 cups skim milk

2 tablespoons part-skim ricotta cheese

Salt and freshly ground pepper to taste

PER SERVING:
Calcium (mg): 201
Fat (g): 1.6
Chol (mg): 40
Carbo (g): 12.2
Protein (g): 13
Calories: 115

Cut the lobster into pieces (see pg. 244) and place in a heavy saucepan with the tomatoes, onion, bay leaf, and basil. Bring to a simmer and cook over low heat for 10 minutes, just until the lobster is cooked (the shells will turn red). Do not overcook.

Remove from heat, take out the lobster pieces, and discard bay leaf. With a small fork, extract the lobster meat from the shells, cut into small pieces, and reserve, discarding shells. (This is a little messy, but worth it.)

Puree the tomato sauce in blender or food processor and pour into a clean saucepan. Add the milk, stir in ricotta, and bring to a simmer. Add the lobster meat, season with salt and pepper, and serve warm.

Makes 6 cups or 4, 1½-cup servings

GREEN GODDESS SOUP

PER SERVING:
Calcium (mg): 291
Fat (g): 1.8
Chol (mg): 3
Carbo (g): 24.3
Protein (g): 9.4
Calories: 146

3 medium new potatoes (about ¾ pound), sliced

1 teaspoon vegetable oil

¼ cup minced onion

2 cups chopped watercress

2 cups chopped fresh parsley

1 cup Chicken Stock or Vegetable Stock (see pg. 247)

¼ teaspoon ground cumin seed

Few dashes cayenne pepper

1 teaspoon dried tarragon

1 leaf fresh basil, chopped, or ¼ teaspoon dried basil

1 cup nonfat dry milk

2 cups water

Salt and freshly ground black pepper to taste

Paprika

Boil the sliced potatoes in their jackets until just tender. Heat the oil in a large nonstick skillet and brown the onion. Add the potatoes, then the watercress, parsley, stock, cumin, cayenne, tarragon, and basil. Cover and simmer 15 minutes. Add the milk mixed with water and simmer 1 minute more.

Remove from heat, let cool, and turn into a food processor, a little at a time, and blend. Add salt and pepper to taste. Serve warm or chilled, with a dash of paprika for garnish. This soup will be tastier after refrigeration.

Makes 6 cups or 4, 1½-cup servings

PINK BORSCHT

3/4 pound beets (makes about 3 cups)

1 cup peeled, seeded, and diced cucumber

2 cups buttermilk

1 tablespoon chopped onion

2 tablespoons fresh, chopped dill or
2 teaspoons dried dill

Dash dried thyme

Salt to taste

1/4 teaspoon freshly ground pepper

1 cup plain low-fat or nonfat yogurt

2 tablespoons vinegar

1 teaspoon fresh lemon juice

Extra yogurt (optional)

PER SERVING:
Calcium (mg): 178
Fat (g): 1.4
Chol (mg): 5
Carbo (g): 13.2
Protein (g): 5.7
Calories: 87

Peel beets, cover with water, and boil until tender, about 30 minutes. Remove from water, cool, and chop fine. Reserve some of liquid to thin soup, if desired. Place cucumber, buttermilk, onion, herbs, and seasoning in food processor and puree. Add chopped beets, then the yogurt, vinegar, and lemon juice. Season again to taste. Serve cold, garnished with dollop of yogurt, if desired.

Makes 6 cups or 6, 1-cup servings

CONNIE'S IOWA BEAN SOUP

PER SERVING:
Calcium (mg): 31
Fat (g): 1.7
Chol (mg): 22
Carbo (g): 17.2
Protein (g): 13.8
Calories: 137

2 cups mixed dried beans, perhaps lima, kidney, and pinto beans, blackeyed and split peas, red lentils, navy beans, garbanzos, etc.

2 tablespoons salt

2 quarts water

2 chicken legs with thighs, skinned

4 tablespoons vinegar

1 large onion, chopped

1 28-ounce can Italian plum tomatoes, broken into pieces

Juice of 1 lemon

1 dried red pepper pod or 1 tablespoon seeded and chopped jalapeño pepper

Salt and freshly ground black pepper to taste

1 teaspoon Durkee's Imitation Bacon Bits

Place beans in large kettle, cover with water and 2 tablespoons salt, and let soak overnight. Replace water several times. When ready to cook, drain, place in kettle with 2 quarts of water, and bring to boil. Add the chicken legs and vinegar, cover, and simmer slowly for 2½–3 hours.

When beans are tender, remove chicken bones from the soup, leaving the meat, and add the onion, tomatoes, lemon juice, and red or jalapeño pepper. Cook, covered, for another 30 minutes. Add salt and pepper and the Bacon Bits, stir, and serve. A sturdy soup for a cool day, nice with salad and cheese for a light supper.

Makes 10 cups or 8, 1¼-cup servings

MEXICAN CORN CHOWDER

1 teaspoon corn oil

1 cup chopped onion

1 clove garlic, minced

¼ cup chopped hot yellow pepper

½ cup chopped green bell pepper

1 cup diced tomatillos (Mexican green tomatoes) or regular green tomatoes

2 cups fresh corn kernels

2 cups Vegetable Stock (see pg. 247)
Salt and freshly ground black pepper to taste

2 cups skim milk

¼ cup diced red bell pepper

PER SERVING:
Calcium (mg): 119
Fat (g): 1.7
Chol (mg): 1.7
Carbo (g): 20.6
Protein (g): 5.8
Calories: 111

Heat oil in nonstick saucepan and cook onion and garlic until translucent. Add hot pepper, green pepper, green tomatoes, corn, and Vegetable Stock. Cook 10–15 minutes. Season with salt and pepper to taste.

Remove about 1–1½ cups of the soup and, after cooling a bit, puree in a food processor. Return to soup pot and add the milk. Heat just to simmer. Pour into warm soup bowls and garnish each with diced red bell pepper.

Makes 6 cups or 6, 1-cup servings

MUSHROOM AND BARLEY SOUP

PER SERVING:
Calcium (mg): 142
Fat (g): 1.7
Chol (mg): 2
Carbo (g): 25.4
Protein (g): 7.4
Calories: 142

3 dried black mushrooms (available in oriental and health food stores)

1 teaspoon safflower oil

1 medium onion, chopped

2 cloves garlic, minced

1 pound mushrooms, sliced

½ cup uncooked barley

3 cups boiling Vegetable Stock (see pg. 247)

2 teaspoons low-sodium soy sauce

2 carrots, sliced

1 teaspoon dried dill weed

½ teaspoon dried thyme

Dash dried marjoram

2 cups skim milk plus 2 tablespoons nonfat dry milk

¼ teaspoon salt

Freshly ground pepper to taste

1 tablespoon chopped fresh parsley

Soften the dried mushrooms in a cup of boiling water for 20 minutes. Heat safflower oil in a large nonstick saucepan and cook onion and garlic until soft. Add sliced mushrooms and stir over low heat for 3 minutes. Drain the dried mushrooms, reserving the liquid (use for thinning soup later, if necessary). Rinse dried mushrooms under cold water, slice thin, and add to pot with remaining ingredients except the parsley. Cook over low heat for about an hour, until barley is tender. Sprinkle a little parsley over each serving.

Makes 7 cups or 7, 1-cup servings

ORIENTAL SNOW PEA SOUP

4 cups Chicken Stock (see pg. 247)

5 ounces tofu (bean curd), cut into 1-inch cubes

1/4 cup minced scallions

1/4 cup thinly sliced mushrooms

1/4 cup finely chopped carrots

1 clove garlic, minced

1 teaspoon grated fresh ginger

Pinch ground anise

1 teaspoon low-sodium soy sauce

1 cup snow peas, trimmed and washed

Extra scallions

PER SERVING:
Calcium (mg): 80
Fat (g): 2.3
Chol (mg): 1
Carbo (g): 7.5
Protein (g): 5.4
Calories: 68

Place all ingredients except the snow peas and extra scallions in a saucepan and bring to a boil. Cover, reduce heat, and simmer until vegetables are tender, about 20 minutes. Add snow peas and cook another minute. Serve with garnish of scallions.

Makes 6 cups or 4, 1 1/2-cup servings

SALMON BISQUE

PER SERVING:
Calcium (mg): 308
Fat (g): 5.8
Chol (mg): 27
Carbo (g): 11.4
Protein (g): 18.8
Calories: 175

1 teaspoon vegetable oil

1/4 cup chopped onion

1/2 cup chopped celery

1/4 cup mashed boiled potato

2 cups skim milk, divided

7 ounces canned pink salmon, with bones and liquid

1 tablespoon chopped fresh dill or 1/2 teaspoon dried dill

Dash cayenne pepper

Salt and freshly ground black pepper to taste

1 tablespoon chopped fresh parsley

Heat oil in nonstick saucepan and cook onion and celery until tender. Stir in potato and 1 cup milk and bring to boil. Add salmon and juice and the remaining milk, mashing the salmon well. Add dill, cayenne, and salt and pepper. Heat until slightly thick and adjust seasoning. Serve in bowls with garnish of fresh parsley. This is a substantial dish and is recommended as a main course, served with a good bread and salad.

Makes 5 cups or 4, 1 1/4-cup servings

SHRIMP CHOWDER

3/4 cup diced celery

3 tablespoons minced onion

1 clove garlic, minced

1 cup Chicken Stock or Vegetable Stock (see pg. 247)

2 4 1/2-ounce cans tiny shrimp or 8 ounces fresh codfish, cut into chunks

1/2 cup nonfat dry milk

1 1/2 cups water

1 cup diced cooked potato

1 tablespoon chopped fresh dill or 1/2 teaspoon dried dill

1 teaspoon curry powder (optional)

Salt and freshly ground pepper to taste

PER SERVING
(using shrimp):
Calcium (mg): 220
Fat (g): 3.4
Chol (mg): 112
Carbo (g): 14.4
Protein (g): 21.3
Calories: 173

PER SERVING
(using codfish):
Calcium (mg): 160
Fat (g): 5.5
Chol (mg): 5.5
Carbo (g): 14.2
Protein (g): 21.3
Calories: 193

Place celery, onion, garlic, and stock in a saucepan and cook until vegetables are tender. Add remaining ingredients and heat. Season to taste.

Makes 5 cups or 4, 1 1/4-cup servings

SQUASH SOUP

PER SERVING:
Calcium (mg): 85
Fat (g): 0.7
Chol (mg): 2
Carbo (g): 12
Protein (g): 3.3
Calories: 62

2 acorn or butternut squash or 1 pumpkin (equal to 3 cups pulp)

$\frac{1}{2}$ cup chopped onion

2 cups Chicken Stock (see pg. 247)

$\frac{1}{2}$ teaspoon ground cinnamon

$\frac{1}{4}$ teaspoon ground coriander

$\frac{1}{4}$ teaspoon ground cumin

$\frac{1}{8}$ teaspoon turmeric

Freshly ground pepper to taste

1 tablespoon apple cider vinegar

1 cup buttermilk

4 tablespoons nonfat dry milk

1 tablespoon low-sodium soy sauce

1 tablespoon chopped fresh parsley

Halve the squash or pumpkin and discard seeds. Slice and place in steamer basket over boiling water. Cover and steam about 20 minutes. Let cool and peel. There should be about 3 cups of pulp. Place pulp in a saucepan with the onion and Chicken Stock. Cook for 10 minutes, cool, then pour into a blender or food processor and puree. Return to saucepan and add the spices, vinegar, milks, and soy sauce. Bring to a gentle simmer. Adjust seasoning and serve in bowls with garnish of parsley.

Makes 6 cups or 6, 1-cup servings

SUMMER SOUP

½ cup peeled and diced potatoes
½ cup sliced carrots
½ cup chopped fresh spinach
½ cup fresh green peas
½ cup cauliflower florets
1 tablespoon arrowroot
1 ½ cups skim milk, divided
¼ teaspoon cayenne pepper
    Salt and freshly ground black pepper
    to taste
1 tablespoon minced fresh parsley

PER SERVING:
Calcium (mg): 143
Fat (g): 0.4
Chol (mg): 2
Carbo (g): 16.9
Protein (g): 5.6
Calories: 90

In a medium saucepan, bring to a boil 2 cups water with a pinch of salt and add the potatoes and carrots. Cover and cook 10 minutes. Add the remaining vegetables and cook another 5 minutes. In the meantime, make a paste of the arrowroot and 3 tablespoons of milk. Add to remaining milk and stir into the vegetables. Add cayenne and simmer another 5 minutes, until vegetables are tender. Season with salt and pepper to taste. Serve with garnish of fresh parsley.

Makes 4 cups or 4, 1-cup servings

TOMATO SHORBA

PER SERVING:
Calcium (mg): 200
Fat (g): 1.6
Chol (mg): 6
Carbo (g): 12
Protein (g): 6.3
Calories: 86

4 cups buttermilk

2 cups canned Italian plum tomatoes

1 tablespoon fresh lemon juice

2 tablespoons chopped scallion

1 tablespoon chopped fresh basil or
1 teaspoon dried basil

1 teaspoon curry powder

Dash white pepper

1 tablespoon chopped fresh parsley

Blend together all ingredients except parsley in a food processor. Serve cold with garnish of fresh parsley.

Makes 6 cups or 6, 1-cup servings

TURKISH YOGURT SOUP

PER SERVING:
Calcium (mg): 92
Fat (g): 2.1
Chol (mg): 49
Carbo (g): 18
Protein (g): 5.6
Calories: 113

4 cups Chicken Stock (see pg. 247)

½ cup uncooked brown rice

Freshly ground pepper

1 cup plain low-fat yogurt

2 eggs (1 yolk only), beaten

1 tablespoon chopped fresh mint or
1 teaspoon dried, crushed mint

1 tablespoon minced fresh parsley

Bring Chicken Stock to a boil in a large saucepan and add the rice and pepper. Cover and simmer for 30 minutes or until rice is tender. Stir yogurt into a bowl with the beaten eggs. To this add ¼ cup of the soup and mix. Return this mixture to the soup in the saucepan and stir. Do not let mixture boil or the yogurt will separate. Serve garnished with dusting of mint and parsley.

Makes 6 cups or 6, 1-cup servings

VICHYSSOISE

1 cup Chicken Stock (see pg. 247)
1 cup peeled and cubed potatoes
1 ½ cups chopped leeks, washed well
2 cups skim milk
2 tablespoons nonfat dry milk
½ teaspoon salt
Dash freshly ground pepper
1 tablespoon part-skim ricotta cheese
1 tablespoon chopped chives

PER SERVING:
Calcium (mg): 233
Fat (g): 2.9
Chol (mg): 11
Carbo (g): 19.2
Protein (g): 7.7
Calories: 133

Place stock, potatoes, and leeks in food processor or blender and process, covered, to liquefy. Pour into a saucepan and cook until potatoes are tender. Put remaining ingredients except chives into blender, add cooked vegetable mixture, and process again until smooth. Pour into a bowl and chill before serving. Top with sprinkling of chives.

Makes 4 cups or 4, 1-cup servings

ZUCCHINI SOUP

PER SERVING:
Calcium (mg): 155
Fat (g): 1.3
Chol (mg): 4
Carbo (g): 11.2
Protein (g): 5.5
Calories: 76

2 cups Vegetable Stock or Chicken Stock (see pg. 247)

2½ cups sliced zucchini

1 cup chopped onion

2 cloves garlic, minced

Dash dried marjoram

1 teaspoon curry powder

Salt and freshly ground black pepper to taste

2 tablespoons nonfat dry milk

1 cup plain low-fat yogurt

1 teaspoon fresh lemon juice

2 tablespoons diced red bell pepper or pimiento

Place ingredients except yogurt, lemon juice, and bell pepper in a medium saucepan and bring to a boil. Reduce heat, skim off any froth that accumulates, cover, and simmer over low heat for 10 minutes or until zucchini is tender. Let cool, then puree in food processor, a little at a time. Add yogurt and lemon juice and chill well. Garnish with red bell pepper or pimiento.

Makes 6 cups or 4, 1½-cup servings

CHAPTER 3 **ENTREES**

Entrees are the mainstay of most meals, unless one is just "grazing" and eating abundant smaller dishes. The main course recipes in this section are varied: some are vegetarian, some have meat, some fish or shellfish, but all of them are filling, delicious, easy to make, and a considerable calcium cache.

Calcium can be augmented by adding extra nonfat dry milk to favorite recipes such as chopped meat, turkey, and dairy dishes. Marinate fish or chicken in skim milk or buttermilk or yogurt before cooking. The best sources of calcium in the main dish department are low-fat cheeses; shellfish such as shrimp, scallops, oysters, and lobster; canned sardines and salmon with their bones; trout; "cream" sauces; sunflower and sesame seeds, almonds and hazelnuts; and tofu and other soybean products.

Many substitutions may be made in these recipes—chicken may be substituted for fish, or vice versa, and lobster for shrimp.

Meal plans should include an attractive combination of colors and textures, with vegetables and carbohydrates and greens providing balanced nutrition.

GOAT'S-CHEESE BURGERS

PER SERVING:
Calcium (mg): 173
Fat (g): 17.8
Chol (mg): 101
Carbo (g): 3.6
Protein (g): 28.9
Calories: 295

1 pound 90% lean ground round steak

$\frac{1}{2}$ teaspoon freshly ground pepper

$\frac{1}{2}$ teaspoon salt

1 tablespoon chopped onion

$\frac{1}{2}$ teaspoon ground coriander

4 tablespoons nonfat dry milk

2 tablespoons chopped fresh parsley

3 ounces goat's cheese (in log shape, cut into 4 equal rounds)

Extra parsley for garnish

Mix all ingredients, except the cheese, together with a fork, but do not overwork. Shape into 4 patties about ¾ inch thick. Grind a little extra pepper onto each side of them and place in preheated broiler about 3 inches from heat source. Broil for 3 minutes, turn, and broil other side for 2 minutes. Pull out broiler pan and top each burger with a goat's cheese round. Return and broil for another 2 minutes, being careful not to let cheese burn. Remove and serve with garnish of parsley sprigs. Nice to serve with color-contrasting foods such as broiled tomatoes, snow peas, or asparagus.

Variation: This may be made with ground turkey instead of beef. It will then be lower in calories.

Serves 4

GREEN NOODLE AND BEEF CASSEROLE

~~~~~~

7 ounces broad spinach or whole wheat noodles

¾ cup low-fat cottage cheese, rinsed under cold water

½ cup part-skim ricotta cheese

¼ cup minced onion

3 tablespoons chopped green bell pepper

1 tablespoon chopped fresh parsley

1 tablespoon drained and chopped pimiento

¾ pound 90% lean ground round steak

1 cup tomato sauce

1 tablespoon chopped fresh basil or 1 teaspoon dried basil

¼ teaspoon dried oregano

1 clove garlic, minced

½ teaspoon crushed hot red pepper

Salt and freshly ground black pepper

Vegetable spray

PER SERVING:
Calcium (mg): 109
Fat (g): 9.8
Chol (mg): 7.3
Carbo (g): 25.5
Protein (g): 22.6
Calories: 284

Cook the noodles according to package directions until just tender; drain and set aside, keeping warm. Mix cottage cheese and ricotta and combine with onion, green pepper, parsley, and pimiento. In a nonstick skillet, brown the meat. Drain off fat and liquid. Add tomato sauce to the meat along with basil, oregano, garlic, hot pepper, and salt and pepper. Stir to combine. Pour a small amount of the meat sauce into the bottom of a vegetable-oil-sprayed 2-quart casserole or two loaf pans. Over the meat, place half the noodles, then the cheese and vegetable mixture, then the remaining noodles. Top with the remaining meat sauce. Bake in preheated 350°F oven for 50 minutes.

Serves 6

LAMB KEBABS IN SPINACH SAUCE

PER SERVING:
Calcium (mg): 258
Fat (g): 13.9
Chol (mg): 88
Carbo (g): 10.8
Protein (g): 31.2
Calories: 294

2 tablespoons vegetable oil

3 tablespoons fresh lemon juice

1/4 cup tarragon vinegar

1 tablespoon crushed garlic, divided

1 pound lean lamb, trimmed of fat, cubed

2 cups finely chopped cooked spinach (2 pounds fresh)

1 teaspoon minced onion

1 tablespoon grated fresh ginger (wash but do not peel)

1 cup plain low-fat yogurt

2 tablespoons nonfat dry milk

Make a marinade of the oil, lemon juice, vinegar, and half the garlic and marinate the lamb for 3 hours, turning to coat. Drain, then thread lamb cubes onto skewers and broil for 5 minutes, turning. In the meantime, heat the spinach in a saucepan and add the remaining garlic, onion, and ginger. Mix in the yogurt and dry milk to make a sauce of medium thickness. Briefly heat, but do not boil. Remove lamb from skewers, pour sauce over meat, and serve. Nice with brown rice or sweet potatoes.

Serves 4

RICOTTA VEAL LOAF

1 1/2 pounds lean ground veal
1/4 cup nonfat dry milk
1 tablespoon chopped fresh parsley
1 small onion, chopped
1 clove garlic, minced
Salt and freshly ground pepper to taste
1/2 teaspoon dried oregano
1/2 teaspoon dried basil
1/4 cup grated Parmesan or sapsago cheese
1 cup part-skim ricotta cheese
1 egg white, beaten

PER SERVING:
Calcium (mg): 137
Fat (g): 9.8
Chol (mg): 76
Carbo (g): 3.2
Protein (g): 22.5
Calories: 197

Preheat oven to 350°F. Mix together the veal, nonfat dry milk, parsley, onion, garlic, salt and pepper, herbs, and grated cheese. Blend the ricotta with the egg white. Place half the meat mixture into a loaf pan and spread the ricotta mixture over it. Top with remaining meat. Seal the edges to keep ricotta from escaping. Bake, uncovered, for 45 minutes.

Serves 8

VEGETABLE VEAL STEW

PER SERVING:
Calcium (mg): 142
Fat (g): 12.1
Chol (mg): 91
Carbo (g): 15.2
Protein (g): 29
Calories: 303

1 teaspoon safflower oil

1 cup coarsely chopped onion

2 cloves garlic, minced

1 pound stewing veal, trimmed of fat and cut into 1-inch cubes

2 tablespoons arrowroot

1 1/2 cups Chicken Stock (see pg. 247)

1/4 cup chopped fresh parsley

1 cup chopped carrot

1/2 pound mushrooms, sliced

1 bay leaf

1/2 teaspoon dried dill

1 teaspoon Hungarian sweet paprika

Salt and freshly ground pepper to taste

1/4 cup dry white wine

1 cup plain low-fat yogurt

Heat oil in a nonstick saucepan and sauté onion and garlic. Add meat and brown. Remove meat and onions and keep warm. Stir arrowroot into the pan and cook until smooth. Add Chicken Stock and stir to blend. Return meat and onions to saucepan, add all remaining ingredients except yogurt, and cook until meat is tender, about 1½ hours. Adjust seasoning. Remove bay leaf, stir in yogurt, and heat until just warm. Stir and serve with brown rice pilaf or spinach noodles.

Serves 4

CHICKEN À LA KING

1 teaspoon Best Butter (see pg. 249)

¼ cup chopped celery

1 cup sliced mushrooms

1½ cups Basic White Sauce (see pg. 249)

1 cup diced cooked chicken

¼ cup chopped and drained canned pimientos

¼ cup slivered blanched almonds

2 tablespoons dry sherry (optional)

Salt and freshly ground pepper

4 slices whole wheat toast, crusts trimmed, cut into triangles

PER SERVING:
Calcium (mg): 168
Fat (g): 13.2
Chol (mg): 52
Carbo (g): 23.2
Protein (g): 20.5
Calories: 298

Heat Best Butter in large nonstick skillet or saucepan and sauté the celery and mushrooms. Drain and set aside, keeping warm. Make the white sauce and add to it the mushrooms, celery, chicken, and pimientos, stirring to combine. Add the almonds and sherry and adjust seasoning. Place toast triangles on warm plates and spoon the creamed chicken over them. Nice with a green vegetable such as broccoli or asparagus.

Serves 4

MOZZARELLA CHICKEN ROLLUPS

PER SERVING:
Calcium (mg): 205
Fat (g): 9.1
Chol (mg): 82
Carbo (g): 4
Protein (g): 32.3
Calories: 243

1 pound (4) skinless and boneless chicken breast halves, pounded flat

Salt

1 teaspoon Dijon mustard

4 large or 8 small leaves fresh sage

4 ounces part-skim mozzarella cheese, cut into 4 slices

1 teaspoon safflower oil

1/2 cup chopped onion

1 cup sliced mushrooms

Freshly ground pepper

1 tablespoon chopped fresh parsley

1/4 cup dry white wine

Preheat oven to 350°F. Trim chicken breasts of all fat and sprinkle with a little salt. Spread ¼ teaspoon mustard on each. Place 1 large or 2 small sage leaves and 1 slice of cheese on each. Roll up to make little bundles and seal edges with small skewer or toothpicks.

Heat the oil in a nonstick skillet and cook onions until translucent. Brown chicken rolls lightly. Transfer to a baking dish and top with mushrooms, pepper, parsley, and wine. Cover and bake for 30 minutes.

Serves 4

MURGI CHICKEN CURRY

1 tablespoon vegetable oil

2 large onions, chopped

2 cloves garlic, minced

5 teaspoons curry powder

1 pound skinless and boneless chicken breasts, cut up

1 ½ cups plain low-fat yogurt

2 tomatoes, seeded and chopped

PER SERVING:
Calcium (mg): 192
Fat (g): 8
Chol (mg): 71
Carbo (g): 14.8
Protein (g): 30.8
Calories: 258

Heat oil in large nonstick skillet and sauté onions and garlic. Stir in curry powder. Brown chicken pieces in skillet. Mix in the yogurt and tomatoes. Bring to a boil, then lower heat and cook gently until chicken is tender, about 10 minutes. Serve over brown rice or boiled potatoes with a cucumber-sprouts or green pepper vegetable dish.

Serves 4

SAUTÉED CHICKEN WITH YOGURT

1 tablespoon vegetable oil

1 pound (4) skinless and boneless chicken breast halves, all fat removed

1 small onion, minced

1 clove garlic, minced

1 tablespoon arrowroot

1 cup evaporated skim milk

1/2 cup water

1/2 teaspoon freshly grated nutmeg

Salt and freshly ground pepper to taste

1 1/2 cups plain low-fat yogurt

2 tablespoons finely chopped fresh parsley

Heat oil in a nonstick skillet and sauté chicken until lightly browned. Remove chicken and keep warm. In same pan, cook onion and garlic until translucent. Then add the arrowroot and cook over low heat, stirring. Remove from heat. Mix evaporated skim milk and water and add to the skillet gradually, stirring with a whisk. Return to heat and continue stirring. Cook for a minute, until the sauce has reached a boil. Season with nutmeg and salt and pepper. Stir in yogurt. Add sautéed chicken and simmer over low heat, covered, 45 minutes. Serve with garnish of chopped parsley.

Serves 4

SPINACH CHICKEN BAKE

4 medium red potatoes (about 1 pound)

1 pound (4) skinless and boneless chicken breast halves

1 tablespoon oil

1/2 cup chopped onion

1 clove garlic, minced

1 pound fresh spinach, trimmed, steamed, drained, and chopped

1/4 teaspoon freshly grated nutmeg

Vegetable spray

1 cup plain low-fat yogurt

2 tablespoons fresh lemon juice

1/2 teaspoon salt

Freshly ground pepper to taste

1 tablespoon chopped fresh parsley

PER SERVING:
Calcium (mg): 230
Fat (g): 4.7
Chol (mg): 70
Carbo (g): 22.4
Protein (g): 33
Calories: 260

Wash but do not peel potatoes. Cut them into bite-sized pieces and boil in saucepan until tender but still firm. Meanwhile, brown the chicken cutlets in a nonstick skillet in 1 tablespoon of oil. Remove when browned and set aside. Sauté onion and garlic in same skillet. Blend the spinach with the onions and garlic and stir in nutmeg.

Drain the potatoes and combine with spinach mixture. Coat a large casserole with vegetable oil spray and turn the mixture into it. Arrange the chicken on top. Mix the yogurt with lemon juice, salt, and pepper and spoon over the chicken. Sprinkle with parsley, cover, and bake 45 minutes in preheated 350°F oven.

Serves 4

TURKEY DIVAN

PER SERVING:
Calcium (mg): 230
Fat (g): 4.7
Chol (mg): 70
Carbo (g): 22.4
Protein (g): 33
Calories: 260

2 cups cut-up fresh broccoli

1 tablespoon Best Butter (see pg. 249)

1 tablespoon arrowroot

2 tablespoons minced onion

1 cup skim milk

1 tablespoon dry sherry

$\frac{1}{2}$ teaspoon Dijon mustard

$\frac{1}{8}$ teaspoon cayenne pepper

$\frac{1}{2}$ cup grated part-skim mozzarella cheese

1 teaspoon minced fresh parsley

2 cups cubed cooked turkey breast

2 tablespoons grated Parmesan or sapsago cheese

Blanch broccoli, drain, and arrange in bottom of ovenproof casserole. In a saucepan, heat Best Butter and add arrowroot. Cook about 1 minute, then add onion and cook over low heat. Mix the milk with sherry, mustard, and cayenne. Gradually add to saucepan, stirring until slightly thickened. Add grated mozzarella cheese and parsley and cook until the cheese melts. Add turkey and blend thoroughly. Pour mixture over the broccoli, sprinkle with grated Parmesan, and bake in preheated 350°F oven until top is brown and bubbling, about 35 minutes. Nice with spinach noodles.

Serves 6

TURKEY STROGANOFF

1 pound ground turkey

1 teaspoon vegetable oil

½ cup minced onion

2 cloves garlic, minced

2 cups sliced mushrooms (about ½ pound)

2 tablespoons arrowroot

¾ cup chicken broth

¾ cup red wine

½ teaspoon salt

Pinch Hungarian sweet paprika

1 teaspoon poppy seeds

1 cup low-fat plain yogurt

PER SERVING:
Calcium (mg): 134
Fat (g): 10
Chol (mg): 64
Carbo (g): 13.8
Protein (g): 30.1
Calories: 308

In a large nonstick skillet, brown the turkey, then remove, drain, and reserve. In same pan, heat the oil, add onion and garlic, add mushrooms, and cook until soft. Stir in the arrowroot, then the broth and wine. Bring to simmer and stir until sauce thickens. Add salt, paprika, and poppy seeds and mix. Return turkey to the skillet and simmer about 5 minutes. Remove from heat, stir in yogurt, and serve with potatoes, rice, or noodles.

Serves 4

BAKED BLUEFISH DULSE

PER SERVING:
Calcium (mg): 176
Fat (g): 3.4
Chol (mg): 58
Carbo (g): 7.4
Protein (g): 26.8
Calories: 193

Vegetable spray

4 bluefish fillets, about 1 1/2 pounds

1 cup Yogurt Sour Cream (see note below)

1 tablespoon low-sodium soy sauce

1/3 cup minced green onions

1 teaspoon grated fresh ginger (washed but unpeeled)

1 teaspoon Dijon mustard

2 tablespoons dulse or nori (or any dried seaweed available in health food stores or oriental markets)

1 tablespoon chopped fresh parsley

Preheat oven to 450°F. With vegetable oil spray, coat a baking dish large enough to hold fish. Wash and pat dry the fish fillets and place in baking dish. Mix remaining ingredients except the seaweed and parsley and spread over the fish. Bake, uncovered, on highest rack for 10–15 minutes. Toast seaweed by passing it over stove top burner; then crumble it. Garnish fish with sprinkling of the toasted seaweed and chopped parsley.

Note: To make 1 cup plain Yogurt Sour Cream, follow recipe for Yogurt Sour Cream (see pg. 254), using 2 cups plain nonfat or low-fat yogurt.

Serves 4

INDIAN FISH BAKE

1/4 cup nonfat dry milk

2 cups hot mashed potatoes

Vegetable spray

1 cup plain low-fat yogurt

1 pound (2 cups) flaked, cold cooked fish such as cod, haddock, or snapper

1 green chili, minced

1 small onion, minced

1 tablespoon minced fresh parsley or watercress

1/2 teaspoon salt

Dash freshly ground pepper

Paprika

1/4 cup chopped chives

PER SERVING:
Calcium (mg): 217
Fat (g): 9.9
Chol (mg): 87
Carbo (g): 21.3
Protein (g): 31.4
Calories: 303

Mash the dry milk into the potatoes, adding water to thin, if necessary, then turn half the mixture into a vegetable-sprayed casserole. Mix the yogurt with the fish, chili, onion, parsley, and salt and pepper. Spread over the potatoes. Top with remaining potatoes. Sprinkle with paprika and bake in preheated 350°F oven for 15 minutes, until top is browned. Sprinkle chives over top and serve.

Serves 4

CRAB GRATIN

PER SERVING:
Calcium (mg): 163
Fat (g): 8.7
Chol (mg): 96
Carbo (g): 10.8
Protein (g): 19
Calories: 231

Vegetable spray

2 tablespoons Best Butter (see pg. 249)

2 tablespoons minced shallots

1/2 pound lump or backfin crabmeat

Salt and freshly ground pepper

1/4 teaspoon dried tarragon, crushed

1/3 cup dry vermouth

1/2 cup evaporated skim milk

1 tablespoon arrowroot

4 tablespoons nonfat dry milk

1/2 teaspoon tomato paste

Dash fresh lemon juice

2 tablespoons grated Parmesan or sapsago cheese

Paprika

Coat 4 scallop shells or 1, 8-inch gratin dish with vegetable oil spray. Heat Best Butter in a nonstick skillet and cook shallots. Add crab, salt, pepper, and tarragon and cook for 2 minutes, stirring. Add vermouth, turn up heat and boil, stirring, until liquid has nearly evaporated. Remove from heat.

In a small bowl, mix 3 tablespoons of evaporated milk with arrowroot and beat in remaining milk, dry milk, and tomato paste. Add to crab mixture and return to moderate heat. Bring to simmer and cook about 2 minutes, stirring. If sauce is too thick, add more milk. Adjust seasoning and add dash of lemon juice.

Spoon crab mixture into the shells or gratin dish and sprinkle tops with grated cheese. Sprinkle with paprika and place under broiler for 5 minutes, until cheese browns. Remove and serve with a simple bread and salad.

Serves 4

62   The High-Calcium Low-Calorie Cookbook

LOBSTER NEWBURG

1 tablespoon Best Butter (see pg. 249)

1 tablespoon arrowroot

1 ½ cups evaporated skim milk

2 cups cooked lobster meat (see pg. 244)

½ teaspoon salt

Dash white pepper

¼ teaspoon paprika

¼ teaspoon freshly grated nutmeg

2 tablespoons dry sherry

¼ cup chopped fresh parsley

PER SERVING:
Calcium (mg): 74
Fat (g): 3.8
Chol (mg): 41
Carbo (g): 5.8
Protein (g): 10.6
Calories: 104

Heat Best Butter in nonstick saucepan and add arrowroot, stirring for a few minutes until blended. Add the milk, stir, and cook until smooth. Add lobster pieces, spices, and sherry and cook until just thickened. Serve over brown rice or noodles with garnish of chopped parsley.

Serves 4

QUICK OYSTER STEW

PER SERVING:
Calcium (mg): 216
Fat (g): 12.1
Chol (mg): 91
Carbo (g): 10.5
Protein (g): 15.1
Calories: 212

16 fresh oysters

¼ cup clam juice

2 tablespoons whipped butter

2 dashes celery salt

2 teaspoons low-sodium soy sauce

1 cup skim milk

1 cup evaporated skim milk

Paprika

1 teaspoon chopped fresh parsley

Freshly ground pepper (optional)

Heat 2 soup bowls before starting this quick dish. Make certain oysters are fresh; they should be tightly closed when purchased. Shuck oysters (see pg. 244) and reserve liquid from them. Place the oysters, ½ cup reserved oyster liquid, clam juice, butter, celery salt, and soy sauce in the top of a double boiler set over boiling water. Stir briskly for 1 minute until oysters plump up and edges begin to curl. Add the skim milk and evaporated skim milk, stir briskly, and remove from heat just before liquid reaches the boil. Ladle into the hot bowls and garnish each with a dusting of paprika and parsley. Season with pepper if desired. Serve with plain oyster crackers.

Serves 2

CONFETTI SALMON MOUSSE

1 envelope plain gelatin

½ cup boiling water

2 tablespoons fresh lemon juice

½ cup chopped onion

¼ teaspoon paprika

1 tablespoon chopped fresh dill or
   1 teaspoon dried dill

2 dashes cayenne pepper

1 cup nonfat or low-fat plain yogurt

2 cups canned pink salmon with skin and
   bones, drained

¼ cup diced red and green bell peppers

2 cups fresh spinach leaves, romaine, or
   other salad greens

½ cup alfalfa sprouts

PER SERVING:
Calcium (mg): 355
Fat (g): 7.5
Chol (mg): 42
Carbo (g): 9
Protein (g): 27.4
Calories: 215

Pour gelatin powder into food processor and add boiling water, lemon juice, onion, paprika, dill, and cayenne and puree for 1 minute. Add yogurt and mix until just blended. Mash salmon and bones and stir into yogurt mix.

Scatter the mixed red and green peppers around the bottom of a ring mold and pour salmon mixture into the mold. Chill until ready to serve. To unmold, place form in a hot water bath for a minute or so and then turn onto a platter lined with greens. Place alfalfa sprouts in center. Serve with sliced tomatoes and cucumbers if desired.

Makes 4 cups or 4, 1-cup servings

POACHED SALMON WITH HORSERADISH SAUCE

PER SERVING:
Calcium (mg): 216
Fat (g): 12.1
Chol (mg): 91
Carbo (g): 10.5
Protein (g): 15.1
Calories: 212

1 small onion, quartered
6 black peppercorns
1 bay leaf
2 slices lemon
4 salmon fillets, about 1 pound
1/4 cup minced fresh dill
1/4 cup freshly grated horseradish
   Freshly ground pepper to taste
1 teaspoon fresh lime juice
1 teaspoon Dijon mustard
1 cup plain low-fat yogurt
   Parsley or dill sprigs

Fill a large, deep skillet with 2 inches of water, bring to a boil, and add onion, peppercorns, bay leaf, and lemon. Let boil 5 minutes. Lower heat to simmer and slide in the salmon fillets. Cover and poach gently for 5 minutes. Remove from bouillon (save it as fish stock, strained, for later use). Chill the fish before serving.

In the meantime, combine the remaining ingredients except parsley or dill sprigs and set aside for 30 minutes or more. When ready to serve, spoon some of the sauce onto the serving plate and place salmon over it. Serve rest of sauce separately. Garnish with parsley or a sprig of dill.

Note: Other fish fillets such as mackerel, bluefish, or swordfish may be substituted.

Serves 4

SALMON CROQUETTES

1 ½ cups canned pink salmon, with bones

3 cups peeled and cooked potatoes (about 1 pound), mashed

¼ cup diced green bell pepper

2 tablespoons minced scallions

½ teaspoon paprika

1 egg white, beaten

Dash cayenne pepper

½ teaspoon dried dill weed

½ teaspoon mustard

Freshly ground black pepper to taste

¼ cup wheat germ

1 tablespoon vegetable oil

Mushroom Cream Sauce (see pg. 249)

Chopped fresh parsley

PER SERVING:
Calcium (mg): 99
Fat (g): 7.5
Chol (mg): 21
Carbo (g): 11.4
Protein (g): 10.4
Calories: 150

Mash together first 10 ingredients and shape into croquettes or patties. Spread wheat germ on flat surface and roll croquettes in it until coated. Heat oil in nonstick skillet and brown croquettes on all sides. Serve with 1 tablespoon Mushroom Cream Sauce per patty and sprinkling of parsley.

Makes about 10 patties or 5, 2-patty servings

SALMON LOAF EVELYN

PER SERVING:
Calcium (mg): 258
Fat (g): 0.6
Chol (mg): 39
Carbo (g): 15.6
Protein (g): 26.7
Calories: 242

1/2 cup quick oats

15 ounces canned pink salmon with
bones, drained

4 tablespoons plain low-fat or nonfat yogurt

1 teaspoon fresh lemon juice

1 tablespoon minced onion

1 tablespoon chopped fresh dill or
1 teaspoon dried dill

Few dashes cayenne pepper

Vegetable spray

6 pimiento-stuffed olives, sliced

3 tablespoons Grape-Nuts

Mix together all ingredients except vegetable spray, olives, and Grape-Nuts. Coat a loaf pan with vegetable spray, then line with olive slices. Turn salmon mixture into pan, sprinkle Grape-Nuts on top, and bake, covered, in a preheated 400°F oven for 30 minutes. Turn out onto platter to serve.

Serves 4

SALMON-STUFFED PEPPERS

15 ounces canned pink salmon with bones, drained

1 cup shredded low-fat Cheddar cheese or Formagg (see pg. 239)

¼ cup grated sapsago or Romano cheese

3 medium green bell peppers

3 medium red bell peppers

1 teaspoon vegetable oil

1 cup minced onion

1 clove garlic, chopped

1½ cups drained and chopped canned Italian plum tomatoes

1 teaspoon dried oregano, crumbled

¼ teaspoon freshly ground black pepper

Dash cayenne pepper

2 tablespoons wheat germ

PER SERVING:
Calcium (mg): 389
Fat (g): 8.4
Chol (mg): 53
Carbo (g): 13.3
Protein (g): 25.4
Calories: 277

Combine drained salmon and bones with the cheeses. Slice tops off peppers and remove seeds and rough white ribs. Chop tops of peppers and add to oiled nonstick skillet along with the onion and garlic. Cook until tender, then add tomatoes, oregano, and black and cayenne peppers. Cook for 2 minutes more, mixing well. Add to salmon and cheese mixture.

Stuff the peppers, top with sprinkling of wheat germ, and place them in ovenproof casserole containing about ½ cup of water. Cover with foil and bake in preheated 350°F oven for 30–40 minutes.

Serves 6

COQUILLES ST. JACQUES

PER SERVING:
Calcium (mg): 349
Fat (g): 5.5
Chol (mg): 79
Carbo (g): 13.6
Protein (g): 36.2
Calories: 255

1 cup Chicken Stock (see pg. 247)

2 scallions, sliced

5 peppercorns

2 cups bay scallops (1 pound)

3 tablespoons dry vermouth or sherry

2 tablespoons arrowroot

2 tablespoons nonfat dry milk

½ cup buttermilk

1 teaspoon fresh lemon juice

Dash cayenne pepper

Vegetable spray

1 cup sliced mushrooms (½ pound)

½ cup grated low-fat cheese (skim-milk mozzarella or Muenster)

1 tablespoon wheat germ

2 tablespoons chopped fresh parsley

In a saucepan, bring stock to simmer with scallions and peppercorns and cook for 10 minutes. Strain and return liquid to pot. Add scallops and cook, covered, for 1–2 minutes. Remove scallops and keep warm. Add vermouth or sherry to the saucepan and boil down to 1 cup.

In the meantime, mix together arrowroot, dry milk, and buttermilk. Slowly add to stock sauce with lemon juice and cayenne.

Coat scallop shells or casserole with vegetable oil spray, and spoon into them equal portions of mushrooms and scallops, covering each with sauce. Top with grated cheese and wheat germ. Place shells on cookie sheet and bake in preheated 350°F oven for 10 minutes. Then quickly pass under broiler to brown. Garnish with chopped parsley.

Serves 4

RED AND GREEN SCALLOP DELIGHT

1 pound large sea scallops

1 ½ cups tomato sauce

1 teaspoon (or less) crushed hot red pepper

1 clove garlic, minced

½ teaspoon minced fresh ginger

1 tablespoon chopped green bell pepper

2 scallions, chopped

3 cups fresh broccoli florets

2 cups quartered fresh tomatoes

Chopped fresh parsley

PER SERVING:
Calcium (mg): 260
Fat (g): 12.6
Chol (mg): 78
Carbo (g): 28.2
Protein (g): 41.5
Calories: 363

Slice scallops in half horizontally and reserve. Heat tomato sauce in large skillet and add hot red pepper, garlic, ginger, green pepper, and scallions. Stir to combine.

Blanch the broccoli, remove from pot, and drain. Drop scallops and tomatoes into the sauce and stir, cooking about 3–5 minutes. Arrange broccoli around outer rim of a deep serving dish and spoon scallops with sauce into the middle of the plate. Garnish with parsley.

Serves 4

SCALLOP AND OYSTER SALAD

PER SERVING:
Calcium (mg): 258
Fat (g): 12
Chol (mg): 58
Carbo (g): 11.7
Protein (g): 24.8
Calories: 240

1 teaspoon minced shallot

1 tablespoon wine vinegar

Salt and freshly ground white pepper to taste

$1/4$ teaspoon mustard

3 tablespoons fresh lemon juice

1 tablespoon olive oil

2 cups loosely packed, shredded spinach, well washed and spun dry (about $1/2$ pound fresh spinach leaves)

1 cup finely shredded radicchio or red leaf lettuce

2 small tomatoes, peeled, seeded, and cut into $1/2$-inch pieces

10 fresh sea scallops, rinsed, dried, and sliced in half

12 fresh oysters, shucked (see pg. 244)

1 tablespoon chopped fresh parsley

Combine the shallot, vinegar, salt, pepper, mustard, and lemon juice in a small bowl. Slowly stir in oil until blended. Toss the spinach with half the dressing and place on 4 salad plates. Toss the radicchio with remaining dressing and arrange over spinach. Place the tomato pieces on top of the spinach in little mounds.

Broil the scallops for 2 minutes, turning to cook on both sides. Set a steamer basket over boiling water and steam the oysters, covered, for 1 minute, until their edges curl. Remove and arrange both scallops and oysters decoratively on the 4 plates. Sprinkle tops with garnish of chopped parsley and a dash of white pepper. Nice with a good bread for a light supper or luncheon.

Serves 4

CURRIED SHRIMP AND SCALLOPS

1 small onion, chopped

1/2 cup chopped green bell pepper

Vegetable oil

1 tablespoon Best Butter (see pg. 249)

1 tablespoon arrowroot

1 cup evaporated skim milk

2 tablespoons nonfat dry milk

2 teaspoons curry powder

2 tablespoons dry white wine (optional)

1/2 pound medium shrimp, cooked, peeled, and deveined

1/2 pound sea scallops, sliced in half

1/2 cup seeded and chopped fresh tomato

2 tablespoons slivered almonds

1 tablespoon chopped fresh parsley

PER SERVING:
Calcium (mg): 255
Fat (g): 6.9
Chol (mg): 112
Carbo (g): 17.4
Protein (g): 34.4
Calories: 209

In a nonstick skillet, sauté the onion and green pepper in a little oil. Remove from pan and reserve. Heat Best Butter in skillet and blend in arrowroot. Add evaporated milk and dry milk, and stir until sauce thickens. Add curry, wine, shrimp, scallops, sautéed vegetables, and chopped tomatoes and heat through. Serve over hot brown rice with a garnish of almonds and parsley.

Serves 4

GREEN AND WHITE FISH ROLLS

PER SERVING:
Calcium (mg): 174
Fat (g): 10
Chol (mg): 86
Carbo (g): 7.7
Protein (g): 31.1
Calories: 251

1 tablespoon Best Butter (see pg. 249), divided

2 tablespoons minced shallots

4 sole or flounder fillets, about 1 pound

20 green beans or thin asparagus spears

Vegetable spray

1 tablespoon arrowroot

1 cup skim milk

2 tablespoons grated sharp Cheddar cheese ($\frac{1}{2}$ ounce) or Formagg

Salt and freshly ground black pepper to taste

Dash cayenne pepper

2 tablespoons grated Parmesan cheese

Paprika

Chopped fresh parsley

In nonstick skillet, heat 1 teaspoon of Best Butter and sauté shallots. Wash fish fillets and pat dry. Spread browned shallots over fillets. In the meantime, blanch beans or asparagus, drain, and place in equal portions in center of fillets. Roll up fish around vegetables and secure with toothpicks or small skewers. Coat baking dish with vegetable spray and arrange the rolled fillets in dish.

Melt remaining 2 teaspoons Best Butter in a saucepan and stir in arrowroot, blending well. Stir in milk and, when sauce begins to thicken, add Cheddar cheese, salt, pepper, and cayenne. Spoon sauce over the fish fillets, then top with the Parmesan and a sprinkle of paprika. Bake, uncovered, in preheated 350°F oven for 15 minutes or until cheese sauce is bubbly. Run under broiler to brown. Remove, garnish with parsley, and serve.

Serves 4

SOLE FLORENTINE

½ pound fresh spinach, steamed and chopped

½ cup part-skim ricotta cheese

½ cup low-fat cottage cheese

4 tablespoons nonfat dry milk

2 tablespoons chopped fresh parsley, divided

¼ teaspoon freshly grated nutmeg

½ teaspoon salt

Dash freshly ground pepper

8 sole or flounder fillets, about 1 pound

Vegetable spray

2 tablespoons grated Parmesan or sapsago cheese

Paprika

PER SERVING:
Calcium (mg): 210
Fat (g): 10.6
Chol (mg): 91
Carbo (g): 5
Protein (g): 35.4
Calories: 260

Press all excess moisture from the spinach and mix with ricotta, cottage cheese, nonfat dry milk, 1 tablespoon of parsley, and seasonings. Place a generous 2 tablespoons of this filling in the center of each fish fillet. Roll up, fold ends of fish over, and place fillets seam side down, arranged snugly side by side, in a vegetable-oil-sprayed baking dish. Sprinkle with Parmesan or sapsago and garnish with ribbon of remaining parsley and dash of paprika. Bake 45 minutes in preheated 350°F oven.

Serves 4

BASIC PIZZA CRUST

PER SERVING
(crust only):
Calcium (mg): 38
Fat (g): 5.8
Chol (mg): 0
Carbo (g): 29.6
Protein (g): 5.4
Calories: 190

1 1/4 teaspoons active dry yeast
2/3 cup warm (105–115°F) water
2 tablespoons vegetable oil
3/4 teaspoon coarse salt
3 tablespoons nonfat dry milk
3/4 cup whole wheat flour
1–1 1/4 cups all-purpose unbleached flour
Vegetable oil for bowl

In a small bowl, dissolve the yeast in 1/3 cup warm water and let stand 5 minutes, until it bubbles. Stir in the vegetable oil, salt, dry milk, and whole wheat flour until blended. Gradually add unbleached flour to make a rough dough. Turn out on floured surface and knead for about 4 minutes, adding more unbleached flour as necessary to make a soft dough.

Lightly oil a large bowl and place the dough in it, turning to coat all sides. Cover and place in draft-free warm place for 3–4 hours, until dough has tripled in bulk. Punch down dough and roll out on floured surface to form a 12-inch circle. Top with any of the following fillings.

Note: Dough may be allowed to rise for 2 hours, punched down, and refrigerated or frozen, tightly wrapped. When ready to use, remove from freezer, let thaw, unwrap, and let rise for 2 hours in a warm place; then proceed as in basic recipe.

Serves 6

Ratatouille Topping

1 teaspoon olive oil

$\frac{1}{2}$ cup chopped onion

1 clove garlic, minced

$\frac{1}{2}$ cup diced eggplant

$\frac{1}{2}$ cup chopped zucchini

1 medium ripe tomato, peeled, seeded, and chopped (about 1 cup)

2 tablespoons minced fresh parsley

1 tablespoon chopped fresh basil or 1 teaspoon dried basil

1 teaspoon dried oregano

Salt and freshly ground pepper to taste

$\frac{1}{2}$ cup grated part-skim mozzarella cheese

PER SERVING:
Calcium (mg): 113
Fat (g): 8.1
Chol (mg): 6
Carbo (g): 32.9
Protein (g): 8.4
Calories: 134

Heat oil in nonstick skillet and sauté onion and garlic. Add eggplant and zucchini and cook about 5 minutes. Add tomato, herbs, and salt and pepper, and cook until vegetables are tender. Spread over a 12-inch pizza crust. Sprinkle mozzarella over the topping and bake in preheated 400°F oven 25–30 minutes.

Serves 6

Shrimp and Leek Topping

PER SERVING:
Calcium (mg): 171
Fat (g): 9.4
Chol (mg): 14
Carbo (g): 37.5
Protein (g): 9.5
Calories: 269

¼ cup Vegetable Stock (see pg. 247)

2 cups thinly sliced leeks, well washed

2 tablespoons grated Parmesan or sapsago cheese

1 large ripe tomato, peeled, seeded, and diced

¼ pound medium shrimp, shelled and deveined

Bring Vegetable Stock to simmer and lightly cook leeks in it. Sprinkle grated Parmesan or sapsago over pizza crust, then top with drained leeks and tomato. Bake 15–20 minutes in preheated 400°F oven, remove from oven, and arrange shrimp on top. Bake 5 minutes more, until the shrimp turn pink and are cooked through.

Serves 6

Mozzarella, Tomato, and Sardine Topping

PER SERVING:
Calcium (mg): 290
Fat (g): 12
Chol (mg): 46
Carbo (g): 33.1
Protein (g): 17.2
Calories: 307

2 cups peeled, seeded, and diced tomatoes

1 8-ounce can sardines in tomato sauce

4 ounces part-skim mozzarella, grated

2 tablespoons grated Parmesan or sapsago cheese

Arrange tomatoes over pizza crust, top with the sardines and sauce, then sprinkle on the mozzarella and Parmesan. Bake 25–30 minutes in preheated 400°F oven.

Serves 6

FLORENTINE LASAGNA ROLLUPS

12 ripple-edged lasagna noodles

1 tablespoon vegetable oil

¾ cup chopped onion

2 10-ounce packages frozen chopped spinach, thawed and drained

½ teaspoon freshly grated nutmeg

½ teaspoon salt

Freshly ground pepper to taste

½ cup plain low-fat yogurt

4 ounces shredded part-skim mozzarella cheese

1 tablespoon Best Butter (see pg. 249)

1 tablespoon arrowroot

1 cup evaporated skim milk

½ cup skim milk

2 teaspoons Vogue Instant Chicken Flavored Base

¼ cup grated Parmesan or sapsago cheese

PER SERVING:
Calcium (mg): 174
Fat (g): 4.7
Chol (mg): 9
Carbo (g): 21.4
Protein (g): 8.2
Calories: 159

Preheat oven to 350°F. Cook the lasagna noodles in boiling water according to package directions until just tender (usually about 12 minutes). Drain and set aside, flat. Heat oil in a large nonstick skillet and sauté onions. Mix in the spinach, spices, yogurt, and mozzarella and set aside. In the meantime, melt Best Butter in a saucepan, add the arrowroot, and cook about 1 minute, stirring until smooth. Pour in evaporated milk and skim milk and blend until creamy (see directions for Basic White Sauce, pg. 249). Add the Chicken Flavored Base and stir until dissolved. Remove from heat.

Spread a little of the sauce in a 9 by 13-inch baking dish. Then spoon about ¼ cup of the spinach mixture on each lasagna noodle and roll up in jelly roll fashion. Place filled noodles alongside each other in the baking dish. Pour remaining sauce on top and sprinkle with the cheese. Bake for 30–35 minutes, until hot and bubbly.

Serves 6 (two rollups per person)

TOFU SOBA NOODLE BAKE

8 ounces buckwheat soba noodles or 2 cups cooked Basic Brown Rice (see pg. 248)

Vegetable spray

1 teaspoon safflower oil

½ cup chopped onion

2 cloves garlic

¼ cup chopped fresh parsley, divided

½ teaspoon grated fresh ginger

½ cup chopped red bell pepper

1 cup chopped bok choy

8 ounces tofu (bean curd), drained and mashed

¼ cup Ricotta Peanut Butter (see pg. 178)

1 teaspoon slivered lemon zest

Cook soba noodles in boiling water until tender (only 3–5 minutes). Drain and turn into a vegetable-oil-sprayed 1½-quart casserole. Heat the oil in a nonstick skillet and sauté the onion. Mince the garlic together with 2 tablespoons of parsley and add to skillet with ginger. Add bell pepper and bok choy and cook a few minutes, stirring to combine. Add mashed tofu and blend. Place the tofu and vegetable mixture over the noodles and top with Ricotta Peanut Butter. Bake in preheated 350°F oven for about 25 minutes. Remove from oven, top with remaining parsley, and garnish with lemon zest.

Serves 4

MUSHROOM MANICOTTI

6 manicotti shells

1 pound fresh spinach

1 tablespoon vegetable oil

1 small onion, chopped fine

1 clove garlic, minced

6 ounces fresh mushrooms, rinsed and sliced

1 egg white

1 cup part-skim ricotta cheese

3/4 cup grated part-skim mozzarella cheese

2 tablespoons grated Parmesan or sapsago cheese

1/2 teaspoon freshly grated nutmeg

1/2 teaspoon salt

Dash freshly ground pepper

Vegetable spray

3 ounces tomato paste

1 cup water

Pinch each of dried basil, thyme, oregano, and rosemary

PER SERVING:
Calcium (mg): 396
Fat (g): 10.6
Chol (mg): 30
Carbo (g): 33.1
Protein (g): 19.3
Calories: 300

Preheat oven to 375°F. Cook manicotti shells as directed on package, about 10–12 minutes, until tender, then drain. Wash the spinach well, trim, and steam. Drain and chop fine. Heat oil in a nonstick skillet and lightly sauté onions and garlic. Add mushrooms and cook until liquid is released. Drain. Beat the egg white until stiff but not dry. In a large separate bowl, mix ricotta, mozzarella (reserving some for topping), Parmesan or sapsago, spinach, sautéed vegetables, and spices. Fold egg white into ricotta mixture. Stuff the shells and place in a vegetable-oil-sprayed baking dish. Combine the tomato paste, water, and herbs and pour over shells. Sprinkle with remaining mozzarella. Bake, uncovered, for 35 minutes.

Serves 6

PASTA PRIMAVERA

1 tablespoon Best Butter (see pg. 249)

1 tablespoon arrowroot

1 cup evaporated skim milk

2 tablespoons chopped parsley

1 clove garlic, minced

½ teaspoon salt

Dash cayenne pepper

1 cup green peas, blanched

1 cup broccoli florets, blanched

1 cup sliced mushrooms

1 pound spinach pasta (rotelles, shells, or shape of your choice)

1 cup cherry tomatoes

2 tablespoons grated Parmesan or sapsago cheese

Fresh black pepper to taste

Make Basic White Sauce of first three ingredients (see pg. 249). Add chopped parsley, garlic, salt, cayenne, and vegetables, except for tomatoes. Cook, stirring, until mixture just reaches boiling and remove from heat. Cook the pasta until tender, about 8 minutes. Drain, toss with the vegetable sauce and tomatoes. Sprinkle on cheese and pepper and toss.

Serves 12

MACARONI, TOMATO, AND CHEESE CASSEROLE

8 ounces elbow macaroni (whole wheat preferred)

1 tablespoon Best Butter (see pg. 249)

1 tablespoon arrowroot

3 cups skim milk

¾ cup grated part-skim mozzarella cheese

¼ cup grated Romano or sapsago cheese

¼ cup grated Cheddar cheese or Formagg

1 teaspoon grated onion

1 teaspoon mustard

½ teaspoon salt

Freshly ground pepper

4 medium tomatoes, peeled and sliced

Chopped fresh parsley

PER SERVING:
Calcium (mg): 326
Fat (g): 7.4
Chol (mg): 21
Carbo (g): 25.2
Protein (g): 13.4
Calories: 221

Cook macaroni in boiling water to which a little oil has been added until just tender, about 8 minutes. Drain, run under cold water, and place in mixing bowl.

In nonstick skillet, melt Best Butter and blend in arrowroot to form a paste. Add milk and stir until it thickens. Add the cheeses, onion, mustard, salt, and pepper and cook, stirring, until cheese melts. Remove from heat and mix with macaroni.

Place half of the mixture in ovenproof casserole and top with half the tomato slices. Repeat layering, then bake in preheated 350°F oven for 20 minutes. Pass under broiler until cheese sauce bubbles. Remove from oven, sprinkle with chopped parsley, and serve.

Serves 8

TORTELLINI IN CHEESE SAUCE

PER SERVING:
Calcium (mg): 276
Fat (g): 10.5
Chol (mg): 24
Carbo (g): 29.6
Protein (g): 11.7
Calories: 262

2 tablespoons Best Butter (see pg. 249)

2 tablespoons arrowroot

2 cups skim milk

2 tablespoons nonfat dry milk

Salt and freshly ground black pepper to taste

1/8 teaspoon freshly grated nutmeg

1/8 teaspoon cayenne pepper

1/4 cup cubed part-skim mozzarella or Swiss cheese

15 ounces fresh cheese-filled tortellini

Vegetable spray

2 tablespoons grated Parmesan cheese

Melt Best Butter in a nonstick saucepan and add arrowroot, stirring to blend. Add the skim and dry milk and stir with wooden spoon until sauce thickens. Add seasonings and then the cubed cheese. Heat, stirring, until cheese melts.

In the meantime, preheat oven to 450°F, and in a large saucepan bring to a boil 2 quarts of lightly salted water. Drop tortellini into water and cook until tender, 5–7 minutes. Drain and turn into vegetable-oil-sprayed baking dish. Spoon cheese sauce over tortellini and sprinkle with Parmesan. Bake for 10 minutes and quickly run under broiler to brown.

Serves 4

HOT TAMALE PIE

1 teaspoon safflower oil

1 cup chopped onion

1 cup chopped green bell pepper

¼ cup chopped celery

1¾ cups canned Italian plum tomatoes, crushed

1 10-ounce package frozen whole kernel corn

2 cups canned red kidney beans, rinsed and drained

3 teaspoons (or less) crushed hot red pepper flakes

4 cups Vegetable Stock (see pg. 247)

1½ cups yellow cornmeal

½ cup plus 2 tablespoons nonfat dry milk

Vegetable spray

¼ cup shredded sharp Cheddar cheese (or Formagg)

½ cup shredded part-skim mozzarella cheese

PER SERVING:
Calcium (mg): 171
Fat (g): 4.2
Chol (mg): 9
Carbo (g): 43.5
Protein (g): 12.5
Calories: 256

Heat the oil in a large nonstick skillet and cook onion, bell pepper, and celery until tender. Add tomatoes, corn, kidney beans, and crushed red pepper. Cook, uncovered, for about 15 minutes, until thick, stirring to combine. In another saucepan, heat the Vegetable Stock. Stir in the cornmeal and nonfat dry milk and cook, stirring constantly, until thick and smooth. Remove from heat. Coat a deep 9-inch square baking pan (or 2 smaller casseroles) with vegetable oil spray. Pour in the cornmeal mixture, then the bean and tomato sauce. Combine the shredded cheeses and sprinkle on top of the pie. Bake in preheated 350°F oven for 40–45 minutes, until bubbly.

Serves 6–8

NICE RICE PIE

PER SERVING:
Calcium (mg): 257
Fat (g): 7.6
Chol (mg): 66
Carbo (g): 10.2
Protein (g): 13.4
Calories: 164

1 teaspoon vegetable oil

6 ounces fresh mushrooms, sliced

Vegetable spray

1 cup Basic Brown Rice (see pg. 248)

2 eggs (1 yolk only), beaten

½ cup low-fat cottage cheese

½ cup part-skim ricotta cheese

¼ cup grated Parmesan or sapsago cheese

½ cup grated part-skim mozzarella cheese (or any low-fat mild cheese)

1 cup Swiss chard, spinach, kale, or a combination, steamed and chopped

Heat vegetable oil in nonstick skillet and sauté mushrooms. Drain. Coat an 8-inch pie pan with vegetable oil spray and press cooked rice into pan to form crust. Mix the remaining ingredients together to blend and spoon over the rice. Bake, uncovered, in preheated 350°F oven for 15 minutes.

Serves 6

BROCCOLI RICOTTA PIE

2 cups part-skim ricotta cheese

2 eggs, beaten

1 cup chopped broccoli florets and some stems

6 leaves spinach or chard, well washed

1/4 cup finely chopped onion

2 tablespoons chopped fresh basil or 1 teaspoon crumbled dried basil

1 tablespoon whole wheat flour

1 tablespoon all-purpose unbleached flour

1/2 cup grated part-skim mozzarella cheese

Cayenne, nutmeg, and freshly ground pepper to taste

1 unbaked Perfect Pie Crust (see pg. 252)

Paprika

PER SERVING:
Calcium (mg): 273
Fat (g): 13.5
Chol (mg): 94
Carbo (g): 18.2
Protein (g): 15
Calories: 250

Mix all ingredients except crust and paprika together. Turn into the unbaked pie shell and sprinkle with paprika. Bake in preheated 375°F oven for 40–45 minutes.

Serves 8

MEATLESS MOUSSAKA

PER SERVING:
Calcium (mg): 198
Fat (g): 7.7
Chol (mg): 19.8
Carbo (g): 13.4
Protein (g): 9.5
Calories: 171

1 medium eggplant

Salt

1 tablespoon vegetable oil

1 cup chopped onion

2 cloves garlic, minced

8 ounces mushrooms, sliced

1/4 cup chopped fresh parsley

2 stalks celery, chopped

1 cup canned Italian plum tomatoes

1/2 cup dry red wine

1 teaspoon dried mint, crumbled

1/4 teaspoon ground cinnamon

1/2 teaspoon dried thyme

Salt and freshly ground pepper to taste

1 cup part-skim ricotta cheese

1 egg

1/4 cup grated Parmesan or sapsago cheese

1 teaspoon dried basil

Vegetable oil

Preheat oven to 350°F. Peel and slice the eggplant. Sprinkle lightly with salt and drain. Heat oil in a skillet and brown the onion and garlic. Add mushrooms, parsley, celery, tomatoes, wine, mint, cinnamon, thyme, and salt and pepper. Simmer until liquid is absorbed. In a separate bowl, mix together the ricotta, egg, half the Parmesan, and basil. Coat a casserole with vegetable oil and layer in it half the eggplant, half the tomato mixture, and half the cheese mixture. Repeat layers and top with remaining Parmesan. Bake, uncovered, for 45 minutes.

Serves 6

TOFU FRITTATA

3–4 medium-size leeks, well washed
    and trimmed

1 cup chopped Swiss chard

1 cup tofu (bean curd)

½ cup low-fat cottage cheese

¾ cup skim milk

2 tablespoons arrowroot

½ teaspoon low-sodium soy sauce

Salt and freshly ground pepper to taste

3 tablespoons grated Parmesan or
    sapsago cheese

Paprika

PER SERVING:
Calcium (mg): 198
Fat (g): 7.7
Chol (mg): 19.8
Carbo (g): 13.4
Protein (g): 9.5
Calories: 171

Preheat oven to 350°F. Slice cleaned leeks into ¼-inch rings. Steam leeks and chard. Drain. Set aside. Combine remaining ingredients except the Parmesan and paprika in a food processor and blend until smooth. Place vegetables in a 9-inch pie pan and pour tofu mixture over them. Sprinkle with grated cheese and a dash of paprika for color. Bake, uncovered, for 20–30 minutes, until nicely browned.

Serves 6

TOFU PARMESAN

PER SERVING:
Calcium (mg): 323
Fat (g): 13.6
Chol (mg): 17
Carbo (g): 11.1
Protein (g): 15.8
Calories: 222

2 cakes firm tofu (bean curd) (2 cups)

1 teaspoon vegetable oil

1 cup chopped onion

1 cup chopped green bell pepper

10 ounces tomato sauce

1 cup chopped mushrooms

Dash cayenne pepper

Vegetable spray

3 tablespoons chopped fresh oregano or
2 teaspoons dried, crumbled

6 ounces part-skim mozzarella cheese,
cut into thin slices

2 tablespoons grated Parmesan or
sapsago cheese

1 tablespoon wheat germ

Cut tofu into ½-inch slices and press in paper toweling to remove excess moisture. Heat oil in a nonstick skillet and sauté onion. Add green pepper, tomato sauce, and mushrooms and bring to simmer. Cook over low heat for 20 minutes. Add cayenne and stir.

Place half the tofu slices in a layer in a vegetable-oil-sprayed 8-inch baking dish; then layer half the oregano, mozzarella, tomato sauce, and grated cheese. Repeat layering until all ingredients are used up. Sprinkle on the wheat germ and bake, covered with foil, in a 350°F oven for 30 minutes or until cheese is melted.

Serves 6

APPLE PANCAKES

$\frac{1}{2}$ cup part-skim ricotta cheese

$\frac{1}{2}$ cup low-fat cottage cheese

1 cup grated peeled apple, packed tight

1 tablespoon concentrated frozen orange juice

1 teaspoon fresh lemon juice

2 tablespoons chopped dried figs

$\frac{1}{4}$ cup chopped almonds and hazelnuts

Dash freshly grated nutmeg

Dash ground cinnamon

2 eggs (1 yolk only), beaten

$\frac{3}{4}$ cup whole wheat flour

Vegetable spray

PER SERVING
(3 pancakes without toppings):
Calcium (mg): 153
Fat (g): 9.5
Chol (mg): 79
Carbo (g): 34.9
Protein (g): 4.1
Calories: 269

Mix together all ingredients except flour and vegetable spray. Gradually stir in whole wheat flour. Lightly spray a nonstick griddle and heat until a drop of water bounces off it. Use about ¼ cup of batter for each pancake. Spoon onto griddle and cook until bubbles form, then flip, flatten out, and brown on other side. Keep warm. Serve with extra dollop of yogurt and fresh fruit, Saucy Orange Chiffon (see pg. 178), or any other creamy topping.

Yields 12 pancakes

PUFFY PANCAKES

PER SERVING
(3 pancakes without berries):
Calcium (mg): 193
Fat (g): 4.2
Chol (mg): 74
Carbo (g): 23
Protein (g): 15.9
Calories: 192

1 cup low-fat cottage cheese

1 egg yolk

2 tablespoons nonfat dry milk

1 tablespoon concentrated frozen orange juice

½ teaspoon baking powder

½ cup whole wheat flour

Vegetable spray

2 egg whites, beaten until stiff

1 tablespoon sunflower seeds or sesame seeds

½ cup orange-flavored Yogurt Sour Cream (see note below)

Berries (optional)

In a blender, mix together cottage cheese, egg yolk, dry milk, orange juice concentrate, baking powder, and flour. Add a bit of water to thin batter. Coat a nonstick skillet with vegetable oil spray and heat until a drop of water bounces when sprinkled on pan.

In the meantime, fold beaten egg whites into batter. Use 2 tablespoons of batter to form each pancake (use 1 tablespoon if smaller pancakes are preferred). When bubbles form on top of the pancakes, sprinkle a few sunflower or sesame seeds on each and flip over to brown on the other side. Top with Yogurt Sour Cream and berries, if desired, or use yogurt mixed with sugar-free conserve.

Note: To make ½ cup orange-flavored Yogurt Sour Cream, follow recipe for Yogurt Sour Cream (see pg. 254), using 1 cup plain nonfat or low-fat yogurt and 1 tablespoon concentrated frozen orange juice.

Yields 12 pancakes

BEAUTIFUL BLINTZES

Crepes

1 tablespoon (more if needed) Best Butter (see pg. 249)

1 egg

1 ½ cups buttermilk

½ cup plain low-fat yogurt

½ cup unbleached all-purpose flour

½ cup whole wheat flour

PER 1-CREPE SERVING
(before filling):
Calcium (mg): 58
Fat (g): 2.1
Chol (mg): 26
Carbo (g): 9.4
Protein (g): 3.2
Calories: 68

Heat a nonstick griddle pan and coat with some Best Butter. Mix remaining ingredients until smooth and pour about ¼ cup batter onto griddle, tilting to spread batter thinly. Cook quickly over high heat, turning until lightly browned on each side. Repeat to make 12 crepes. (To freeze, place crepes between sheets of plastic wrap; defrost before proceeding with filling.) If not freezing crepes, stack carefully or arrange on platter before filling (see following pages).

Yields 12 crepes

Cheese Filling

Vegetable spray

2 cups low-fat cottage cheese

1 teaspoon pure vanilla extract

1 teaspoon ground cinnamon

$\frac{1}{4}$ cup raisins

12 crepes

Coat a baking dish with vegetable oil spray. Preheat oven to 375°F. Combine all ingredients and spoon about 2 tablespoons on each crepe. Fold sides and edges together to make tight bundle. Place side by side in baking dish and bake for 20 minutes. Sprinkle tops with additional cinnamon. If desired, top with dab of Great Grape Jelly or Saucy Orange Chiffon (see pg. 178).

Fills 12 blintzes

Apple Filling

Vegetable spray

2 cups finely chopped peeled apples

1 tablespoon arrowroot

$\frac{1}{4}$ cup orange juice

$\frac{1}{2}$ teaspoon ground cinnamon

$\frac{1}{4}$ cup plain low-fat yogurt

1 teaspoon concentrated frozen orange juice

8 crepes

1 tablespoon grated orange zest

Preheat oven to 375°F and coat baking dish with vegetable oil spray. Combine apples, arrowroot, orange juice, and cinnamon and cook in a saucepan until the apples are just soft. Combine the yogurt and orange juice concentrate and reserve. Spoon about 2 tablespoons of the apple mixture, onto each crepe and fold the edges together to seal. Place them in baking dish side by side and bake for about 20 minutes. Serve with a dollop of orange yogurt garnished with sprinkling of orange zest.

Fills 8 blintzes

Blueberry-Cheese Filling

Vegetable spray

1 ½ cups fresh blueberries, picked over and rinsed

1 tablespoon arrowroot

2 teaspoons crystalline fructose

½ cup low-fat cottage cheese

½ cup part-skim ricotta cheese

½ teaspoon ground cinnamon

8 crepes

PER SERVING
(1 filled blintz):
Calcium (mg): 110
Fat (g): 3.6
Chol (mg): 31
Carbo (g): 15.8
Protein (g): 6.9
Calories: 120

Preheat oven to 375°F and coat a baking dish with vegetable oil spray. Combine 1 cup of blueberries with arrowroot and fructose in a saucepan and cook until slightly thickened. Mix together the cottage cheese, ricotta, and cinnamon. Place 1 tablespoon of the cheese mixture and 1 tablespoon of the blueberry sauce on each crepe. Seal the edges tightly and place blintzes side by side in baking dish. Bake about 20 minutes. Garnish with the remaining berries.

Fills 8 blintzes

FRENCH TOAST TREAT

PER SERVING:
Calcium (mg): 88
Fat (g): 1.8
Chol (mg): 3.1
Carbo (g): 14.2
Protein (g): 5.8
Calories: 93

2 egg whites

½ cup skim milk

2 tablespoons nonfat dry milk

½ teaspoon pure vanilla extract

1 teaspoon concentrated frozen orange juice

Ground cinnamon to taste

4 slices whole wheat bread

1 teaspoon Best Butter (see pg. 249)

Beat the egg whites until frothy. Add the milks, vanilla, orange juice, and cinnamon. Dip the bread slices into this and coat well. In a nonstick skillet or griddle, melt the Best Butter and brown the bread. Top with Great Grape Jelly (see pg. 250) or other sugar-free conserve.

Serves 4

WONDERFUL WAFFLES

1 egg
1 cup whole wheat flour
2 tablespoons cornmeal
2 teaspoons crystalline fructose
$\frac{1}{4}$ cup nonfat dry milk
1 cup buttermilk
2 tablespoons safflower oil
2 teaspoons baking powder

PER SERVING:
Calcium (mg): 178
Fat (g): 9.4
Chol (mg): 72
Carbo (g): 31.4
Protein (g): 9.4
Calories: 241

Place all ingredients in blender and process until smooth. Turn into waffle iron and cook according to instructions, removing when brown. Serve with fresh fruit and yogurt or kefir or with sherbet or with Crème Fraîche, Whipped Ricotta Cream, or a dessert sauce (see Chapter 8).

Makes 4 double waffles or 4 servings

BUTTERMILK BLUEBERRY BAKE

⅓ cup whole wheat flour

⅓ cup all-purpose flour

2 teaspoons baking powder

2 tablespoons concentrated frozen orange juice

1 tablespoon crystalline fructose

1 cup buttermilk

Vegetable spray

2 cups fresh blueberries, picked over and rinsed

Orange-flavored Yogurt Sour Cream (see pg. 254) or part-skim ricotta (optional)

Mix together the flours, baking powder, orange juice concentrate, and fructose and gradually add buttermilk, stirring until blended. Coat an 8-inch baking dish with vegetable oil spray and pour in batter. Top with blueberries and place in preheated 350°F oven until puffy and lightly browned, 40–45 minutes. Top with Yogurt Sour Cream or ricotta, if desired.

Serves 6

OATMEAL SOUFFLÉ

3 cups skim milk, divided
1 cup rolled oats
1 teaspoon baking powder
½ teaspoon salt
½ tablespoon crystalline fructose
2 tablespoons walnut oil
3 eggs (only 1½ yolks), separated
Vegetable spray
1 tablespoon sunflower seeds
Ground cinnamon

PER SERVING:
Calcium (mg): 273
Fat (g): 11.9
Chol (mg): 106
Carbo (g): 30
Protein (g): 14.9
Calories: 286

Pour 2 cups of the skim milk into a saucepan and heat to boiling. Add the oats and simmer until thickened, stirring. Remove from heat and add the baking powder, salt, fructose, walnut oil, and remaining cup of milk. Beat the egg yolks into the oatmeal. Beat egg whites until they stand in peaks and fold into oatmeal mixture.

Coat a 1-quart soufflé dish with vegetable oil spray and preheat oven to 350°F. Turn batter into the soufflé dish, sprinkle sunflower seeds on top, and bake for 30–35 minutes, until puffy and lightly browned. Sprinkle with cinnamon and serve. Nice served for breakfast, brunch, or lunch with fresh fruit.

Serves 4

CHEESE AND TOFU SOUFFLÉ

PER SERVING:
Calcium (mg): 376
Fat (g): 27.4
Chol (mg): 18
Carbo (g): 15.6
Protein (g): 17.4
Calories: 193

Vegetable spray

3 slices whole wheat bread, halved

6 ounces firm tofu (bean curd), cut into $\frac{1}{2}$-inch-thick slices

4 ounces grated part-skim mozzarella cheese, sliced

1 $\frac{1}{2}$ cups skim milk

2 egg whites, beaten

2 tablespoons miso (see pg. 241)

1 teaspoon chopped jalapeño pepper

$\frac{1}{2}$ teaspoon celery salt

$\frac{1}{4}$ teaspoon onion powder

1 teaspoon toasted sesame seeds

4 cherry tomatoes, halved

Lightly coat a 1-quart casserole with vegetable oil spray and layer the bread, tofu slices, and cheese, repeating until all ingredients are used. Combine in a separate bowl the milk, egg whites, miso, pepper, celery salt, and onion powder. Pour into casserole and let stand 1–2 hours. Sprinkle top with sesame seeds and place the tomatoes around the perimeter.

Place a shallow pan of water, large enough to hold the casserole, in the oven. Preheat oven to 350°F and put casserole in the pan of boiling water. Bake for about an hour or until sides of the soufflé separate from the casserole dish and top is browned. Replenish water bath as necessary. Remove from oven and serve at once with a salad and fruit, if desired.

Serves 4

COTTAGE CHEESE SOUFFLÉ

1 cup low-fat cottage cheese

2 tablespoons grated Parmesan or sapsago cheese

2 eggs (1 yolk only), separated

$\frac{1}{2}$ teaspoon arrowroot

2 tablespoons evaporated skim milk

$\frac{1}{4}$ teaspoon dried dill weed

$\frac{1}{4}$ teaspoon salt

Dash white pepper

Vegetable spray

Paprika

PER SERVING:
Calcium (mg): 172
Fat (g): 5.5
Chol (mg): 146
Carbo (g): 7.7
Protein (g): 22
Calories: 174

Preheat oven to 350°F. Combine cottage cheese, Parmesan or sapsago (reserve 1 teaspoon), egg yolk, arrowroot, milk, dill weed, and salt and pepper. Beat egg whites until they form stiff peaks. Fold gently into cottage cheese mixture only until blended. Spoon into vegetable-oil-sprayed soufflé dish. Sprinkle remaining Parmesan or sapsago and paprika on top. Bake for 20–25 minutes, until soufflé is puffy and nicely browned. Serve immediately upon removing from oven. Nice with a leafy green salad and toasted bread.

Serves 2

CHAPTER 4 **VEGETABLES**

Mother was on the right track when she said, "Eat your spinach," but she would have been better advised to suggest broccoli, kale, or collards. These green vegetables provide calcium that is more readily absorbed by the body. Okra and turnip tops are also good calcium sources. Many vegetables, such as mustard greens, spinach, Swiss chard, beet tops, parsley, and chives are bound with oxalic acids that often prevent maximum calcium absorption by the digestive system. Some say that cooking will free up the calcium. Small quantities of these greens are certainly recommended. Most are interchangeable: recipes calling for spinach may be made with chard or turnip tops or cabbage. Collards may be cooked with sunflower seeds, nutmeg, cardamom, and other spices. Stir-fried vegetables with various seasonings, sesame seeds, or the addition of soy nuts are healthful and easy to prepare. "Cream" sauce is a high calcium boost for many fresh vegetables. Additional garnishes of bell pepper, shredded cheese, and wheat germ add color and texture.

Select only produce that is brightly colored and unwilted. Fresh vegetables are recommended and have more nutrients than frozen foods. The leafy greens need to be washed carefully: dipped several times in tepid water in the sink and run under cold water. Steam them with just the water remaining on the washed leaves. Discolored leaves and tough stems should be discarded before cooking.

Vegetables may be baked or sautéed in a little oil or Best Butter (see pg. 249), but the best method of cooking to preserve the nutrients is steaming or blanching quickly in boiling water and then draining and running under cold water or plunging into ice water. Do not add baking soda when cooking vegetables. Save the cooking water to make vegetable stock.

Many vegetables may be used raw in salads, and they too can be enhanced by garnishes such as sesame seeds, pimientos, red peppers, shredded carrots, mushrooms, and bean sprouts.

ARTICHOKES

4 globe artichokes
Juice of ½ lemon
1 tablespoon vinegar

PER SERVING
(without sauce):
Calcium (mg): 63
Fat (g): 0.2
Chol (mg): 0
Carbo (g): 13
Protein (g): 3.5
Calories: 35

Cut stems off the artichokes and trim off small leaves at base. Trim about ½ inch off tops and cut points off remaining leaves. Rinse in cold water and rub with lemon juice. Immerse chokes in vinegar and water until ready to cook. In the meantime, bring to a boil 4 quarts of water with some salt. Place artichokes in pot, cover with 2 layers of cheesecloth, and boil, uncovered, for 30–40 minutes, until leaves pull off easily. Drain upside down in a colander. Serve warm or cold with Balsamic Vinaigrette or Lemon Sauce (see pgs. 163, 174).

Serves 4

ASPARAGUS AND PIMIENTO

1 pound fresh asparagus or broccoli
½ cup cold water
1 large pimiento, rinsed and cut into julienne strips
2 tablespoons fresh lime juice
1 tablespoon sesame seeds, toasted

PER SERVING
(using asparagus):
Calcium (mg): 31
Fat (g): 1.1
Chol (mg): 0
Carbo (g): 5.5
Protein (g): 3.3
Calories: 41

PER SERVING
(using broccoli):
Calcium (mg): 130
Fat (g): 1.8
Chol (mg): 0
Carbo (g): 8
Protein (g): 5.4
Calories: 57

Rinse asparagus and snap off tough ends. (If using broccoli, cut into florets.) Bring water to a boil in a large skillet and add asparagus or broccoli. Cover and steam until just tender, 3–4 minutes. Remove from heat, drain, and run under cold water. Arrange on serving platter, decorate with pimiento strips, and sprinkle with lime juice and sesame seeds. Serve warm or chilled.

Serves 4

BOK CHOY

PER SERVING:
Calcium (mg): 64
Fat (g): 3.7
Chol (mg): 0
Carbo (g): 7.1
Protein (g): 1.8
Calories: 63

1 pound bok choy (Chinese celery)
1 tablespoon corn oil
½ teaspoon minced garlic
½ teaspoon crystalline fructose
1 teaspoon low-sodium soy sauce
Few drops sesame oil

Rinse bok choy in cold water. Cut stalks into 1-inch pieces and the leaves into thin shreds. Heat oil in a large nonstick skillet. Add the stems first and sauté, tossing, about 2 minutes. Then add the garlic, bok choy leaves, fructose, soy sauce, and sesame oil and continue cooking over high heat for another 2 minutes. This is also nice served with cooked bean sprouts or mixed with other vegetables.

Serves 4

SESAME BROCCOLI

PER SERVING:
Calcium (mg): 120
Fat (g): 3
Chol (mg): 0
Carbo (g): 11.1
Protein (g): 6.9
Calories: 120

1 pound fresh broccoli, trimmed and cut into florets
1 tablespoon toasted sesame seeds
1 teaspoon sesame oil
1 tablespoon rice wine vinegar
¼ teaspoon hot red pepper flakes
Juice of ½ lemon

Steam broccoli florets over boiling water until tender, 2–3 minutes. Transfer to serving bowl. (Save the pot water for Vegetable Stock [see pg. 247 for recipe].) Combine remaining ingredients and drizzle over warm broccoli.

Serves 4

BROCCOLI AND CAULIFLOWER BAKE

2 cups fresh broccoli florets

2 cups fresh cauliflower florets

Vegetable spray

1 tablespoon Best Butter (see pg. 249)

1 tablespoon arrowroot

1 cup skim milk

2 teaspoons Dijon mustard

Dash onion powder

Freshly ground pepper to taste

2 tablespoons grated sharp Cheddar cheese (or Formagg)

Paprika

PER SERVING:
Calcium (mg): 159
Fat (g): 4.9
Chol (mg): 9
Carbo (g): 12.4
Protein (g): 7.6
Calories: 114

Blanch the broccoli and cauliflower pieces and drain. Place in vegetable-oil-sprayed ovenproof dish. In the meantime, melt Best Butter in nonstick skillet, mix with arrowroot until smooth, then add the milk, mustard, onion powder, and pepper. Stir until sauce becomes thick, then add the cheese and continue stirring until it melts. Spoon sauce over the vegetables, sprinkle with a little paprika, and bake for 15–20 minutes in preheated 350°F oven. Run quickly under broiler to brown.

Serves 4

ONION-CREAMED BRUSSELS SPROUTS

PER SERVING:
Calcium (mg): 104
Fat (g): 1.8
Chol (mg): 2
Carbo (g): 11.7
Protein (g): 6.2
Calories: 78

1 pound Brussels sprouts, trimmed and rinsed

1/4 cup chopped onion

1 clove garlic, chopped fine

1 teaspoon safflower oil

1/2 cup plain low-fat yogurt

2 tablespoons nonfat dry milk

1 tablespoon chopped fresh dill or
1 teaspoon dried dill, crumbled

Drop sprouts into boiling water and cook until tender, about 10 minutes. In the meantime, in nonstick skillet sauté the onion and garlic in heated oil. When sprouts are cooked, drain and mix together with the onions. Remove from heat and add yogurt and milk to the skillet. Sprinkle with fresh or dried dill and serve.

Serves 4

CABBAGE 'N' SPROUTS

1 tablespoon vegetable oil
1 cup sliced onion
1 cup Chicken Stock (see pg. 247)
1 teaspoon salt
1 teaspoon celery salt
3 cups shredded green cabbage
   (about ³⁄₄ pound)
1¹⁄₂ cups bean sprouts, rinsed

PER SERVING:
Calcium (mg): 43
Fat (g): 3.8
Chol (mg): 0
Carbo (g): 8.5
Protein (g): 3
Calories: 73

In nonstick skillet, heat oil and sauté onion in it about 3 minutes. Add the Chicken Stock, salt, and celery salt, mixing well. Then add the cabbage and cook, covered, about 5 minutes. Add sprouts, stir, and cook another 3 minutes, until cabbage is tender but still crisp.

Serves 4

SPICY YOGURT CABBAGE

¹⁄₂ cup minced onion
1 small red cabbage, rough leaves removed, rinsed, and shredded (about 3 cups)
1¹⁄₂ cups peeled and chopped apples
¹⁄₄ teaspoon curry powder
¹⁄₈ teaspoon ground allspice
1 teaspoon salt
1 cup plain low-fat or nonfat yogurt

PER SERVING:
Calcium (mg): 138
Fat (g): 1.2
Chol (mg): 4
Carbo (g): 16.4
Protein (g): 4
Calories: 86

Heat a large nonstick skillet and add the onion and shredded cabbage, cooking until it wilts. Add the apples, spices, and salt and cook another 20 minutes, until the apples are soft. Remove from heat and rapidly stir in yogurt.

Serves 4

HOT COLLARDS

PER SERVING:
Calcium (mg): 184
Fat (g): 6.1
Chol (mg): 1
Carbo (g): 9.8
Protein (g): 5.6
Calories: 103

1 pound collard greens or mustard greens, turnip greens, or kale

2 cups Chicken Stock or Vegetable Stock (see pg. 247)

1 cup fresh chard leaves

3–4 leaves fresh basil

1 tablespoon walnut oil

¾ cup chopped onion

2 cloves garlic, minced

1 tablespoon grated fresh ginger

1 jalapeño pepper, stem and seeds discarded, minced

2 dashes sesame oil

Salt and freshly ground black pepper to taste

1 teaspoon sesame seeds

Wash greens well, dipping into tepid water several times, and slice into thin strips. Place in nonstick pot with the broth, chard, and basil and cook, covered, for about 30 minutes, until greens are tender. In a large nonstick skillet, heat oil and soften onion and garlic in it. Add ginger and jalapeño and stir together. Add collards mixture and stir until liquid is nearly evaporated. Add sesame oil and salt and pepper to taste and stir. When serving, garnish with sprinkling of sesame seeds.

Serves 4

DILLED GREEN BEANS

1 teaspoon safflower oil

2 cloves garlic, minced

1 ½ tablespoons wheat germ

1 tablespoon chopped scallion

1 tablespoon chopped fresh dill or
1 teaspoon dried

1 pound green beans, trimmed (about 3 cups)

3 tablespoons chopped fresh parsley

PER SERVING:
Calcium (mg): 51
Fat (g): 1.4
Chol (mg): 0
Carbo (g): 7.7
Protein (g): 2.4
Calories: 46

In nonstick skillet, heat oil and brown garlic, wheat germ, scallion, and dill. In a medium saucepan, bring to a boil 2 cups water. Drop beans in and cook 3–4 minutes. Drain and run under cold water to stop cooking. Serve warm, topped with dill mixture and parsley.

Serves 4

GREEN BEANS AMANDINE

PER SERVING:
Calcium (mg): 123
Fat (g): 2.8
Chol (mg): 2
Carbo (g): 11.8
Protein (g): 4.5
Calories: 82

1 clove garlic, chopped

2 tablespoons blanched almonds

1/2 cup sliced scallions

1/4 cup minced fresh parsley

1/4 cup fresh lemon juice

Dash cayenne pepper

1 teaspoon Dijon mustard

1/2 cup plain low-fat yogurt

1 pound fresh green beans, trimmed and washed

In a blender, grind the garlic and almonds, then add remaining ingredients except the yogurt and beans. Remove nut mixture from blender and stir into the yogurt. Steam or blanch the beans until just tender, about 5 minutes, then drain. Mix the sauce with the beans in a warm saucepan but do not cook further.

Serves 4

QUICK BRAISED KALE

3 pounds fresh kale

1 tablespoon corn oil

1/2 cup chopped onion

1 clove garlic, minced

1 teaspoon salt

1/4 teaspoon freshly ground pepper

3 tablespoons water

2 teaspoons fresh lemon juice

1 teaspoon Durkee's Imitation Bacon Bits

PER SERVING:
Calcium (mg): 211
Fat (g): 3.3
Chol (mg): 0
Carbo (g): 8.2
Protein (g): 6
Calories: 75

Wash the kale several times and remove tough stems. Chop fine. Heat oil in large nonstick skillet and sauté onion and garlic until brown. Then add kale and remaining ingredients except lemon juice and Bacon Bits. Cook over medium heat for 15–20 minutes, until tender, and then stir in lemon juice and Bacon Bits. Adjust seasoning and serve.

Serves 6

HUNGARIAN KOHLRABI

1 tablespoon Best Butter (see pg. 249)

1 pound kohlrabi (about 6 knobs), peeled and diced

1/2 teaspoon crystalline fructose

4 tablespoons chopped fresh parsley

1/2 cup Chicken Stock (see pg. 247)

PER SERVING:
Calcium (mg): 50
Fat (g): 3.4
Chol (mg): 4
Carbo (g): 7.6
Protein (g): 2.4
Calories: 64

Heat Best Butter in a nonstick skillet and add the remaining ingredients. Cook, covered, for about 30 minutes, until kohlrabi is tender.

Serves 4

LEEKS VINAIGRETTE

PER SERVING:
Calcium (mg): 106
Fat (g): 20
Chol (mg): 1
Carbo (g): 18.5
Protein (g): 2.6
Calories: 97

8 medium leeks, trimmed and well washed
Balsamic Vinaigrette (see pg. 163)

Split the trimmed leeks lengthwise, leaving the white root ends whole. Make certain all sand is rinsed away. Bundle the leeks and tie with string. Drop into a saucepan of boiling salted water and simmer, covered, for about 12 minutes, until just tender. Serve immediately with 1 tablespoon of vinaigrette or place in ice water to stop cooking. Save and freeze the cooking liquid for use in Vegetable Stock (see pg. 247 for recipe).

Serves 4

LADY RAINBOW OKRA

PER SERVING:
Calcium (mg): 100
Fat (g): 2.8
Chol (mg): 0
Carbo (g): 15.5
Protein (g): 4.2
Calories: 97

5 cups tender small okra pods (about 1 pound)

2 egg whites, beaten

1 cup cornmeal

1 tablespoon cayenne pepper

1 tablespoon vegetable oil (or a little more as needed)

Trim ends of okra and cut into ¼-inch slices. Toss pods in egg white to coat. Mix cornmeal and cayenne in a paper bag, drop okra into the bag in small quantities, and shake to coat. Heat oil in a large nonstick skillet and gradually add okra, cooking quickly over high heat until browned.

Serves 6

MARINATED OKRA PODS

1 pound fresh small okra pods, trimmed

¼ cup red wine vinegar

¼ teaspoon salt

2 tablespoons virgin olive oil

1 small red onion, sliced into rings

2 tablespoons fresh lemon juice

Romaine lettuce leaves

2 cups cherry tomatoes

PER SERVING:
Calcium (mg): 107
Fat (g): 4.9
Chol (mg): 0
Carbo (g): 10.7
Protein (g): 3
Calories: 89

Blanch trimmed okra in boiling water for a minute or two, then drain and plunge into ice water to stop cooking. Drain once again and pat dry. In the meantime, mix the remaining ingredients except the lettuce and tomatoes. Pour the marinade into a glass container, add the okra, cover, and refrigerate for a few hours. When ready to serve, drain and place on bed of lettuce with the cherry tomatoes. Top with some of the onion rings, drained.

Serves 6

OKRA

1 pound small fresh okra pods

PER SERVING:
Calcium (mg): 110
Fat (g): 0.4
Chol (mg): 0
Carbo (g): 7.2
Protein (g): 24
Calories: 35

Trim off okra stems and points and rinse under cold water. Drop into pot of boiling water and blanch for 2 minutes. Drain and run under cold water or drop into bowl of ice water to stop cooking. Place on paper toweling to dry. These are now ready to eat, or they may be set aside for use in other dishes. Or add to salads, tomato sauces, or stews. Run quickly under broiler to reheat.

Serves 4

OKRA PROVENÇAL

PER SERVING:
Calcium (mg): 141
Fat (g): 1.6
Chol (mg): 0
Carbo (g): 14.7
Protein (g): 4.3
Calories: 79

1 pound small fresh okra pods, trimmed

12 ounces canned Italian plum tomatoes

4 scallions, chopped

2 cloves garlic, minced

½ cup chopped green bell pepper

8 small pimiento-stuffed olives

4 tablespoons chopped fresh parsley

Pinch each dried thyme and dried marjoram

2 tablespoons chopped fresh basil or
2 teaspoons dried basil, crumbled

Salt and freshly ground black pepper
to taste

Blanch the trimmed okra pods in boiling water for a minute. Drain and run quickly under cold water. Set aside on paper towel until ready to use. In the meantime, place remaining ingredients in a large saucepan and simmer until sauce becomes thick, about 30 minutes. Adjust seasoning. Turn okra into the sauce, stir, and cook until just tender, but not so long that the okra becomes mushy.

Serves 4

PARSNIP PUREE

6 medium parsnips (about 2 cups), peeled
and trimmed

2 tablespoons plain low-fat yogurt

2 tablespoons nonfat dry milk

¼ teaspoon ground mace

¼ teaspoon freshly grated nutmeg

PER SERVING:
Calcium (mg): 79
Fat (g): 0.6
Chol (mg): 1
Carbo (g): 15.2
Protein (g): 2.4
Calories: 73

Cook parsnips in boiling salt water until tender, about 20 minutes. Drain and place in blender or processor to puree, along
with the yogurt and milk. Add the spices and more yogurt if
consistency needs adjusting.

Serves 4

PARIS GREEN PEAS

2 cups shelled fresh green peas (about 1½
pounds in pods) or lima beans

1 tablespoon minced onion

1 tablespoon Best Butter (see pg. 249)

1 cup boiling water

½ teaspoon salt

¼ teaspoon crystalline fructose

2 cups shredded chicory (¼ pound) or
leaf lettuce

1 teaspoon dried mint

PER SERVING
(using peas):
Calcium (mg): 22
Fat (g): 3.4
Chol (mg): 4
Carbo (g): 9.8
Protein (g): 4.1
Calories: 83

PER SERVING
(using lima beans):
Calcium (mg): 36
Fat (g): 3.3
Chol (mg): 4
Carbo (g): 19.1
Protein (g): 6.3
Calories: 128

Wash the peas (or lima beans) and combine in saucepan with
onion, Best Butter, and boiling water. Cover tightly and simmer for
5–10 minutes. Add salt, fructose, and shredded chicory. Stir, cover,
and cook another 2 minutes. Add mint, stir, and serve at once.

Serves 4

RUTABAGA PUREE

PER SERVING:
Calcium (mg): 90
Fat (g): 0.2
Chol (mg): 1
Carbo (g): 11.6
Protein (g): 2.2
Calories: 55

1 rutabaga (about 1 pound), peeled and diced

1 medium potato, peeled and diced

$\frac{1}{4}$ teaspoon cayenne pepper

$\frac{1}{2}$ teaspoon freshly grated nutmeg

4 tablespoons nonfat dry milk

3 tablespoons chopped fresh parsley

Place rutabaga and potato pieces in a saucepan and cover with water. Bring to boil and simmer, covered, for 30 minutes or until vegetables are tender. Reserve some of the water in case the puree needs thinning. Drain and place in a food processor and puree. Add cayenne, nutmeg, and milk and blend. Rewarm in saucepan before serving with a garnish of chopped parsley. This is particularly healthful and colorful if served inside a ring of steamed broccoli florets.

Serves 6

CREAMED SPINACH AND MUSHROOMS

2 pounds fresh spinach, well washed, tough stems trimmed

1 tablespoon Best Butter (see pg. 249)

½ cup trimmed and chopped fresh mushrooms

1 tablespoon minced onion

½ cup evaporated skim milk

½ teaspoon salt

¼ teaspoon freshly ground pepper

Dash freshly grated nutmeg

PER SERVING:
Calcium (mg): 213
Fat (g): 3.6
Chol (mg): 4
Carbo (g): 8
Protein (g): 6
Calories: 78

Place the still wet spinach leaves in a large saucepan and cook over high heat, stirring, until spinach is wilted. Heat Best Butter in a nonstick skillet, add mushroom pieces and onion, and cook about 5 minutes. Add remaining ingredients and heat, stirring. In the meantime, drain the spinach well and chop. Combine with the mushroom sauce and serve.

Serves 4

SPINACH

PER SERVING:
Calcium (mg): 118
Fat (g): 2.7
Chol (mg): 0
Carbo (g): 4.4
Protein (g): 3.6
Calories: 48

1 teaspoon safflower oil

2 cloves garlic, minced

2 pounds fresh spinach (cooks down to 2 cups)

4 dashes sesame oil

2 teaspoons sesame seeds, toasted

In nonstick skillet, heat safflower oil and sauté garlic. Remove from pan and reserve. Wash spinach well, shake off excess moisture, and add to skillet. Cook until wilted, about 5 minutes. Drain off water and toss with garlic and sesame oil. Serve warm or chilled, sprinkled with sesame seeds.

Serves 4

SQUASH AND PEPPERS SALAD

PER SERVING:
Calcium (mg): 52
Fat (g): 2.8
Chol (mg): 0
Carbo (g): 25.3
Protein (g): 4.3
Calories: 123

1 small acorn or butternut squash

3 bell peppers (red, green, yellow, or purple, as available)

1 tablespoon concentrated frozen orange juice

$\frac{1}{3}$ cup fresh lime juice

$\frac{1}{4}$ cup minced fresh mint or 2 tablespoons dried

2 tablespoons chopped toasted almonds

Cut squash in half and steam over boiling water until tender. Peel, seed, and cut into ½-inch slices. Seed the peppers and cut into julienne strips. Combine the orange juice with lime and mint and toss with peppers. Arrange on serving plate with squash slices and garnish with almonds.

Serves 4

YOGURT-STUFFED SQUASH

$\frac{1}{4}$ cup Whole Wheat Bread Crumbs
(see pg. 243)

1 medium carrot, grated (about 1 cup)

$\frac{1}{2}$ teaspoon salt

$\frac{1}{8}$ teaspoon freshly ground pepper

1 cup sliced mushrooms

1 cup minced onion

1 stalk bok choy, chopped fine (about 1 cup)

$\frac{1}{2}$ cup plain low-fat yogurt

2 tablespoons nonfat dry milk

$\frac{1}{8}$ teaspoon ground cumin

2 acorn or butternut squash, split and seeded

PER SERVING:
Calcium (mg): 139
Fat (g): 1.3
Chol (mg): 2
Carbo (g): 29.9
Protein (g): 6.2
Calories: 144

Preheat oven to 350°F. Mix together all the ingredients except the squash. Fill the 4 squash halves with the mixture. Place stuffed squash in a baking dish with a little water in the bottom. Bake for about 40 minutes or until the squash is tender.

Serves 4

QUICK SWISS CHARD

PER SERVING:
Calcium (mg): 113
Fat (g): 3.4
Chol (mg): 4
Carbo (g): 5.4
Protein (g): 2.7
Calories: 57

2 pound fresh Swiss chard (or collard greens, turnip or mustard greens, beet tops, spinach, or broccoli rabe), well washed, stems trimmed

1 teaspoon salt

1 tablespoon Best Butter (see pg. 249)

4 lemon wedges

Trim off any damaged leaves and tough stems of chard. Make sure washing removes all sand. In a saucepan, bring to a boil about ½ inch of water and drop in the chard leaves. When the water boils again, cover and cook 2–3 minutes, until leaves are tender. Add salt and remove from heat. Drain but reserve some of the cooking liquid. Chop the chard, add the Best Butter to the reserved liquid, and pour a little over the chard before serving. Serve each portion with a lemon wedge.

Serves 4

TOMATO AND CHEESE BROIL

2 large tomatoes

4 ounces part-skim mozzarella cheese,
shredded

1 tablespoon olive oil

1 clove garlic, minced

$\frac{1}{4}$ teaspoon dried oregano, crumbled

4 leaves red leaf or romaine lettuce

PER SERVING:
Calcium (mg): 198
Fat (g): 8
Chol (mg): 16
Carbo (g): 5
Protein (g): 8
Calories: 122

Cut each tomato into 4 slices and discard stem ends. Place on rack of a broiling pan. Top each tomato slice with an equal portion of cheese and drizzle mixture of oil, garlic, and oregano over each. Preheat broiler and place tomatoes 4 inches from heat. Broil until cheese begins to bubble and brown. Remove and place on bed of lettuce leaves.

Serves 4

CREAMED VEGETABLES

PER SERVING:
Calcium (mg): 154
Fat (g): 3.3
Chol (mg): 4
Carbo (g): 11.2
Protein (g): 5
Calories: 89

2–3 cups any fresh vegetable or combination, such as asparagus, lima beans, peas, cauliflower, broccoli, cabbage, carrots, celery, turnips, green or wax beans, squash, spinach, or kale

1 cup Basic White Sauce (see pg. 249)

Almonds and hazelnuts

Curry powder or herbs

Grated cheese

Blanch the vegetables and drain before adding the white sauce and seasonings. Use only a few tablespoons of white sauce with the leafy green vegetables.

Variation: To make baked vegetables au gratin, top the vegetables and white sauce with a covering of fresh bread crumbs or wheat germ, a sprinkling of cheese, and a dash of paprika. Bake in pre-heated 350°F oven until browned.

Serves 4

STIR-FRY VEGETABLE MEDLEY

1 teaspoon safflower oil

$\frac{1}{2}$ teaspoon sesame oil

1 tablespoon low-sodium soy sauce

2 cups shredded red cabbage

1 cup shredded green cabbage

$\frac{1}{2}$ cup chopped onion

1 tablespoon finely chopped jalapeño pepper

1 cup broccoli florets

6 leaves spinach or Swiss chard

1 cup Tofu Sauté (see pg. 253), cubed

2 tablespoons toasted pumpkin seeds

PER SERVING:
Calcium (mg): 190
Fat (g): 10.1
Chol (mg): 0
Carbo (g): 13.6
Protein (g): 12.7
Calories: 178

Heat the oils and soy sauce in large nonstick skillet or wok and stir in the vegetables. Cook quickly over high heat, stirring to blend. Add tofu and pumpkin seeds and toss to combine.

Note: Any other vegetables may be used as desired, such as asparagus or green beans.

Serves 2–3

SUMMER SALSA

PER SERVING:
Calcium (mg): 9
Fat (g): 0.1
Chol (mg): 0
Carbo (g): 3.7
Protein (g): 0.7
Calories: 16

1/4 cup chopped onion

1/2 cup chopped green bell pepper

1/2 cup chopped red bell pepper

2 fresh ripe tomatoes, chopped

1/2 cup fresh lemon juice

Freshly ground black pepper

1 tablespoon chopped fresh basil

Mix all ingredients in a small serving bowl and let stand at room temperature about an hour. Stir occasionally and then refrigerate for 1 hour before serving.

Makes 2 cups or 32, 1-tablespoon servings

CHAPTER 5 **GRAINS, NOODLES, AND POTATOES**

Carbohydrates are important in the overall nutritional scheme of things and are necessary for converting our food into energy. High-calcium recipes use brown rice and whole grains such as buckwheat, bulgur, oats, farina, and semolina. The whole grains provide more calcium than refined products. Grains and rice cooked in skim milk provide a lot more calcium.

Potatoes and yams also are vital foods. Whole wheat and vegetable pasta play a role in this calcium compendium as well. Japanese noodles called soba are made of buckwheat flour.

Cook grains and potatoes with a little strip of seaweed for a good calcium and iron boost. Use the skins of potatoes where possible and stuff them with your choice of a creamy filling from Chapters 1, 8, or 12. Wheat germ sprinkled on almost anything is a healthful calcium addition.

Interchange grains for variations on the theme. Prepare them with vegetables, add them to stews, put them in soups, and even use them for desserts.

BRAZILIAN FAROFA

PER SERVING:
Calcium (mg): 107
Fat (g): 4.8
Chol (mg): 1.3
Carbo (g): 16.3
Protein (g): 4.5
Calories: 127

2 cups skim milk
Pinch salt
⅔ cup farina (Cream of Wheat) or Oat Bran
½ cup chopped onion
2 tablespoons chopped red bell pepper
2 tablespoons chopped green bell pepper
2 tablespoons walnut oil
2 tablespoons wine vinegar

In a nonstick saucepan, bring the milk and salt to a simmer. Slowly add the farina, stirring. Let simmer until thickened, about 10 minutes. In the meantime, mix together the onion, red and green peppers, oil, and vinegar. Serve separately as condiment to use over farina or Oat Bran.

Serves 6

BUCKWHEAT GROATS AND VEGETABLES

1 tablespoon safflower oil

2 medium turnips, pared and grated (about 2 cups)

1 medium onion, minced

1 cup sliced mushrooms

½ cup buckwheat groats (kasha)

1 cup skim milk

2 tablespoons nonfat dry milk

2 tablespoons chopped fresh dill or 2 teaspoons dried dill

PER SERVING:
Calcium (mg): 94
Fat (g): 2.9
Chol (mg): 1
Carbo (g): 12.2
Protein (g): 4
Calories: 89

Heat oil in a nonstick skillet and sauté the vegetables. Wash groats, drain, and add to vegetables. Mix and transfer to oven-proof casserole. Combine milks and pour over the mixture and sprinkle with dill. Cover and bake in preheated 350°F oven for 1 hour or until groats are tender. Fluff and serve.

Serves 6

BULGUR AND VEGETABLE CREAM

PER SERVING:
Calcium (mg): 84
Fat (g): 1.8
Chol (mg): 2
Carbo (g): 29.8
Protein (g): 5.2
Calories: 152

1 teaspoon walnut oil

¼ cup chopped onion

1 cup bulgur

½ cup chopped mushrooms

½ cup chopped red cabbage

1 cup grated carrots

1 ½ cups Chicken Stock or Vegetable Stock (see pg. 247)

2 tablespoons chopped dried figs

½ cup plain Yogurt Sour Cream (see pg. 254)

Heat oil in nonstick skillet and cook onion until soft. Add bulgur and cook until it browns, stirring. Add the vegetables (any combination may be used, such as broccoli, peas, green or red cabbage, or bok choy) and stir again to combine. Add the stock and simmer for 20 minutes, until stock is absorbed. Add the figs and the Yogurt Sour Cream. Stir together. Serve warm or chilled. This can also be used as a base for other foods, such as the crust for broiled mozzarella cheese or a frittata.

Makes about 2½ cups or 6 servings

POLENTA AND MUSHROOMS

1 teaspoon olive oil

1 pound mushrooms, cleaned, trimmed, and sliced

2 cups canned Italian plum tomatoes

¼ teaspoon freshly ground pepper

4 cups water, divided

1 cup yellow cornmeal

4 tablespoons nonfat dry milk

4 tablespoons grated Parmesan or sapsago cheese

PER SERVING:
Calcium (mg): 67
Fat (g): 1.8
Chol (mg): 2
Carbo (g): 18.9
Protein (g): 4.8
Calories: 109

Heat olive oil in a nonstick skillet and brown the mushrooms. Slowly stir in tomatoes and pepper. Simmer 15 minutes over low heat. Meanwhile, bring 3 cups of water to a boil in a saucepan. Mix cornmeal with 1 cup of cold water and the non-fat dry milk and gradually stir this into the hot water in the saucepan. Bring back to a boil and cook until thick, stirring constantly. Cover, lower heat, and cook for 10 minutes. Transfer cornmeal to a warm platter, top with the tomato sauce, and sprinkle with grated cheese.

Serves 8

ALMOND RICE PILAF

PER SERVING:
Calcium (mg): 38
Fat (g): 1.7
Chol (mg): 1
Carbo (g): 26.6
Protein (g): 3.4
Calories: 138

1 cup brown rice (basmati if available)

2 cups Chicken Stock or Vegetable Stock (see pg. 247)

½ cup chopped onion

2 tablespoons chopped fresh parsley

2 tablespoons sliced toasted almonds

2 tablespoons grated Parmesan or sapsago cheese

Parsley sprig

Wash rice well under cold water. Bring stock to a boil in medium saucepan and add rice, onion, and parsley. Reduce heat and cook, covered, about 45 minutes, until done. Mix in almonds and cheese. Garnish with parsley sprig. Use any leftovers for pie crust or rice pudding.

Serves 6

RUSSIAN NOODLE PUDDING

8 ounces spinach fettuccini

Vegetable spray

1 cup skim milk plus 2 tablespoons nonfat
dry milk

1 egg white

1 tablespoon concentrated frozen orange juice

½ cup low-fat cottage cheese

2 tablespoons wheat germ

1 tablespoon caraway seeds

1 tablespoon poppy seeds

PER SERVING:
Calcium (mg): 93
Fat (g): 2.2
Chol (mg): 39
Carbo (g): 33
Protein (g): 10.2
Calories: 195

Cook noodles in salted boiling water for 12–14 minutes, until just tender. Drain and place in vegetable-oil-sprayed baking pan. In blender, combine milk, egg white, orange juice concentrate, and cottage cheese. Pour over the noodles and sprinkle them with wheat germ and seeds. Bake in preheated 375°F oven for 15 minutes or until golden.

Serves 6

CREAMED POTATOES GRATIN

PER SERVING:
Calcium (mg): 160
Fat (g): 1.5
Chol (mg): 5.6
Carbo (g): 15.8
Protein (g): 6.2
Calories: 101

2 large potatoes, peeled and sliced thin

½ teaspoon salt

Freshly ground pepper

1 cup skim milk

2 tablespoons nonfat dry milk

2 tablespoons part-skim ricotta cheese

2 tablespoons grated Parmesan or sapsago cheese

Paprika

Bring water to a boil in the bottom of a double boiler. In the top, cook the potatoes with the salt, pepper, and milks for about 30 minutes. Turn into a baking dish, dot the top with mixture of the ricotta and Parmesan cheeses, and sprinkle with paprika. Bake in preheated 350°F oven for 20 minutes.

Serves 4

DUTCH TREAT

1 pound fresh kale or cabbage or other green vegetable, chopped fine (about 7 cups)

4 medium potatoes

½ cup nonfat dry milk combined with ¾ cup water

2 cloves garlic, chopped

6 green onions, chopped

½ cup low-fat cottage cheese

¼ teaspoon salt

Freshly ground black pepper to taste

Dash freshly grated nutmeg

Dash cayenne pepper

PER SERVING:
Calcium (mg): 166
Fat (g): 0.6
Chol (mg): 2
Carbo (g): 19.7
Protein (g): 8
Calories: 112

Rinse the kale well before chopping. Boil potatoes in their jackets until tender. When cooked, slice and return to the saucepan. Spread kale over the potatoes, cover, and steam until tender, 5–7 minutes. Add remaining ingredients and mash together until well blended.

Serves 6

NEW POTATO SALAD

PER SERVING:
Calcium (mg): 88
Fat (g): 1.6
Chol (mg): 2.6
Carbo (g): 17
Protein (g): 6.3
Calories: 107

8 small new potatoes, well scrubbed and cooked until tender

1 cup finely chopped celery

¾ cup plain low-fat yogurt

½ cup low-fat cottage cheese

¼ cup white wine vinegar

1 tablespoon Dijon mustard

1 tablespoon fresh lime or lemon juice

1 tablespoon low-sodium soy sauce

Romaine or spinach leaves

1 tablespoon toasted sesame seeds

Tomatoes or other fresh vegetables for garnish

Slice the potatoes into quarters and place in mixing bowl with the celery. Blend together the remaining ingredients except lettuce, sesame seeds, and garnish, then stir into the vegetables. Chill and serve on bed of romaine or spinach leaves. Sprinkle with sesame seeds and garnish with tomatoes or other fresh vegetables.

Serves 6

POTATO LEEK PIE

2 medium-size new potatoes, well scrubbed and sliced $\frac{1}{4}$ inch thick

1 pound leeks, well washed, trimmed, and cut into $\frac{1}{2}$-inch rounds

$\frac{1}{2}$ cup Chicken Stock or Vegetable Stock (see pg. 247)

Salt and freshly ground black pepper to taste

10 fresh basil leaves, chopped, or 1 table-spoon dried basil, crumbled

Vegetable spray

1 cup sliced mushrooms (about 6 fresh mushrooms)

4 ounces part-skim mozzarella cheese, cubed

Cayenne pepper

PER SERVING:
Calcium (mg): 314
Fat (g): 3.7
Chol (mg): 11
Carbo (g): 14
Protein (g): 10.3
Calories: 120

Boil potato slices until tender, about 15 minutes. Drain. Cook the leeks in the stock until soft and drain. Toss leeks with salt, pepper, and basil. Coat an ovenproof casserole with vegetable oil spray. Fill the casserole with a layer of the potatoes, then the leeks, then mushrooms, and repeat. Top with cheese, press down, and sprinkle with a few dashes of cayenne. Bake, uncovered, for 20 minutes in a preheated 325°F oven.

Serves 6

STUFFED POTATOES

PER SERVING:
Calcium (mg): 119
Fat (g): 1.3
Chol (mg): 4
Carbo (g): 21.2
Protein (g): 5.7
Calories: 118

4 medium baking potatoes, well scrubbed

¼ cup plain Yogurt Sour Cream (see note below)

2 tablespoons nonfat dry milk

2 tablespoons grated Parmesan or sapsago cheese

Snipped chives

Paprika

Prick potatoes in several places with a fork and place in a pre-heated 475°F oven or potato baker. Bake for 1 hour, until shells are very crisp. Remove, cut in half, and scoop out pulp. Mix pulp with Yogurt Sour Cream, dry milk, and cheese. Stuff the shells with the mixture and return to the oven to brown. Serve with a garnish of chives and a dash of paprika.

Note: To make ¼ cup plain Yogurt Sour Cream, follow recipe for Yogurt Sour Cream (see pg. 254), using ½ cup plain nonfat or low-fat yogurt.

Serves 4

SWISS POTATO TORTE

Vegetable spray

4 medium potatoes, peeled and grated coarse (about 2 cups)

2 small onions, grated

1 cup grated low-fat cheese such as Emmenthaler or part-skim mozzarella

1/4 cup grated Parmesan or sapsago cheese

1 teaspoon salt

1/2 teaspoon freshly ground pepper

1/8 teaspoon freshly grated nutmeg

1 tablespoon chopped fresh parsley

Freshly cooked vegetables

PER SERVING:
Calcium (mg): 181
Fat (g): 4.1
Chol (mg): 113
Carbo (g): 14.9
Protein (g): 8
Calories: 127

Coat an 8 x 3½-inch round springform pan with vegetable oil spray. Mix potatoes, onions, cheese, salt, pepper, and nutmeg. Turn into the pan and bake in preheated 450°F oven for 1 hour, until golden brown. Turn the torte out onto a serving platter and garnish with fresh parsley and freshly cooked vegetables.

Serves 6

TURNIP YAM TREAT

PER SERVING:
Calcium (mg): 109
Fat (g): 0.6
Chol (mg): 1
Carbo (g): 32.4
Protein (g): 3.8
Calories: 147

4 turnips, peeled and cubed

2 medium yams, peeled and cubed

1/4 cup nonfat dry milk

1/4 cup water

Few dashes freshly ground pepper

1/4 teaspoon freshly grated nutmeg

Dash dried thyme

2 teaspoons concentrated frozen orange juice

Boil the turnips and yams until tender. Mash together or put through ricer. Add remaining ingredients and stir well together or quickly run through food processor. Adjust seasoning and serve warm. This is especially attractive if served in center of a ring of steamed broccoli.

Serves 4

CHAPTER 6 **SALADS**

Relatively small amounts of calcium are found in the leafy green vegetables, but when served with a low-fat milk-based dressing, a sprinkling of grated cheese, and a garnish of sesame seeds, soy nuts, or sunflower seeds, they add up to calcium-rich salads. Herbs, parsley, chives, finely chopped or julienned vegetables, and perhaps some crumbled seaweed (that's how the Japanese get their calcium!) will also increase the mineral quantity.

Watercress, dandelion greens (those who live in the country have two seasons for these delicious tender weeds as they proliferate in spring and fall), arugula, romaine lettuce, and raw spinach leaves are all fine combinations for your salad bowl, as is radicchio, a red leaf lettuce that is available in Italian and specialty greengrocers and enhances many dishes.

Salad may be served before or after the main dish, or it may comprise the entire meal. Salad is also a nice complement to a hearty soup dish served with tasty bread or muffins.

BELL PEPPER SALAD

PER SERVING:
Calcium (mg): 39
Fat (g): 1
Chol (mg): 1
Carbo (g): 8.3
Protein (g): 2.7
Calories: 37

1 medium red bell pepper

1 medium green bell pepper

1 medium yellow or brown bell pepper

$\frac{1}{2}$ cup Bell Peppers Dressing (see pg. 169)

$\frac{1}{4}$ teaspoon freshly ground black pepper

2 teaspoons rinsed and drained capers

Place peppers under broiler and lightly burn, turning to grill all sides. Remove from broiler and drop into a brown paper bag. Close bag and set aside to let steam a few minutes. When cool, peel and core the peppers and cut into strips. Arrange peppers on a platter, alternating colors so that they form a pinwheel, and pour the dressing over them. Sprinkle with ground pepper, garnish with capers, and serve warm or chilled.

Serves 4

CARROT SALAD

2 cups grated unpeeled raw carrots

¼ cup coarsely chopped dried figs

½ cup plain low-fat yogurt

1 tablespoon concentrated frozen orange juice

1 teaspoon fresh lemon juice

1 teaspoon fennel seed

¼ cup chopped fresh parsley

4 romaine lettuce or spinach leaves

PER SERVING:
Calcium (mg): 108
Fat (g): 0.8
Chol (mg): 2
Carbo (g): 19.7
Protein (g): 3.1
Calories: 91

Mix carrots with chopped figs. Combine yogurt with orange juice concentrate, lemon juice, fennel seed, and parsley. Mix with carrots and figs. Chill before serving on bed of lettuce or spinach.

Serves 4

CHICKEN AND CHEESE SALAD

PER SERVING:
Calcium (mg): 273
Fat (g): 7.4
Chol (mg): 43.8
Carbo (g): 8.2
Protein (g): 19.2
Calories: 171

1 ½ teaspoons minced dried onion

2 tablespoons buttermilk

½ cup plain low-fat yogurt

2 tablespoons part-skim ricotta cheese

¼ cup shredded Jarlsberg or Emmenthaler cheese (1 ounce)

1 teaspoon low-sodium soy sauce

¾ cup diced cooked chicken (or turkey)

½ cup sliced tofu (bean curd), sautéed in nonstick pan

¾ cup sliced bok choy or celery

½ cup shredded carrot

¼ cup chopped green bell pepper

2 tablespoons chopped red bell pepper

8 leaves Swiss chard or spinach

Alfalfa sprouts

1 small ripe tomato, quartered

Soak the dried onion in the buttermilk for 5 minutes, then stir in the yogurt, ricotta, shredded cheese, and soy sauce. Blend well, then combine with diced chicken or turkey. Dice the fried tofu and add it, along with bok choy, carrot, and green and red peppers, to the chicken mixture. Chill until ready to serve, then spoon onto 4 individual plates lined with chard or spinach leaves. Top with garnish of alfalfa sprouts and place tomato quarters alongside each serving. A nice, light, summer luncheon salad.

Serves 4

COMPOSED CHÈVRE SALAD

6 ounces arugula or watercress, trimmed

6 ounces radicchio or curly red lettuce

1 Belgian endive, leaves separated

1 small navel orange, peeled, seeded, and diced

Few thin rounds or diced pieces of carrot

4 ounces goat's cheese

Vegetable spray

Freshly ground black or green pepper

4 tablespoons Balsamic Vinaigrette (see pg. 163)

PER SERVING:
Calcium (mg): 218
Fat (g): 10.3
Chol (mg): 25
Carbo (g): 9.5
Protein (g): 6.5
Calories: 151

Wash salad greens well and pat dry. Arrange attractively on individual salad plates, strewing the orange and carrot pieces over them. Cut cheese into 4 thin slices and place on vegetable-oil-sprayed baking pan. Place under broiler until the cheese begins to melt. Transfer with spatula to top of salads. Sprinkle with pepper and serve with vinaigrette dressing, 1 tablespoon per serving.

Serves 4

DANDELION BLUE CHEESE SALAD

1 pound fresh dandelion leaves (young, tender ones)

$1/4$ cup chopped red onion

$1/2$ cup Blue Cheese Dressing (see pg. 163)

Freshly ground pepper to taste

Wash dandelion greens well in several changes of water and pat dry. Remove coarse stems and tear into 2-inch pieces. Toss with onion and Blue Cheese Dressing and sprinkle with pepper.

Serves 4

GARBANZO SALAD

1 8-ounce can garbanzos (chickpeas), rinsed and drained

½ cup plain Yogurt Sour Cream (see note below)

2 tablespoons fresh lemon juice

2 cloves garlic, minced

⅛ teaspoon cayenne pepper

3 tablespoons chopped fresh mint or 2 teaspoons dried mint

Salt and freshly ground black pepper to taste

4 romaine, spinach, or fresh chard leaves

Few leaves fresh mint or parsley

PER SERVING:
Calcium (mg): 117
Fat (g): 1
Chol (mg): 3.5
Carbo (g): 10.2
Protein (g): 5.3
Calories: 70

Mix the drained garbanzos with the yogurt, lemon juice, garlic, cayenne, mint, and salt and pepper. Chill in covered dish for 1 hour before serving. Place in center of lettuce leaves and garnish with fresh mint or parsley.

Note: To make ½ cup plain Yogurt Sour Cream, follow recipe for Yogurt Sour Cream (see pg. 254), using 1 cup plain nonfat or low-fat yogurt.

Serves 4

MEXICALI BEAN SALAD

PER SERVING:
Calcium (mg): 37
Fat (g): 1.6
Chol (mg): 0
Carbo (g): 16.3
Protein (g): 5
Calories: 93

½ pound fresh green beans, blanched

½ cup drained cooked or canned blackeyed peas or kidney beans

6 ounces Mexican-style corn or 1 cup fresh corn kernels

½ cup drained cooked lima beans

2 small tomatoes, cored and diced

¼ cup thinly sliced red onion

3 tablespoons fresh lime juice

3 tablespoons white wine vinegar

½ teaspoon crystalline fructose

1 teaspoon garlic powder

½ teaspoon dried oregano, crushed

¼ teaspoon hot red pepper flakes, crushed

6 romaine or spinach leaves

2 tablespoons toasted pumpkin seeds

Mix together first six vegetables and refrigerate for a few hours. Combine remaining ingredients for dressing, except romaine and seeds. When ready to serve, place ½ cup vegetables on greens and serve with dressing and sprinkling of pumpkin seeds.

Serves 6

MEXICAN MIXED SALAD

3 tablespoons red wine vinegar

1 tablespoon Dijon mustard

1/4 cup fresh lime juice

Romaine lettuce leaves

1 pound carrots, scraped and grated

1 pound beets, peeled, boiled, drained, and julienned

Beet tops, well washed

1 lime, sliced

PER SERVING:
Calcium (mg): 81
Fat (g): 0.8
Chol (mg): 0
Carbo (g): 26.5
Protein (g): 3.4
Calories: 114

Combine vinegar, mustard, and lime juice. Line salad plates with romaine leaves. Fill with equal portions of carrots and beets. Boil beet tops and drain. Place some of these on the lettuce leaves too. Garnish each dish with a lime slice and serve with the lime mustard dressing.

Serves 4

MIDDLE EAST CUCUMBER SALAD

PER SERVING:
Calcium (mg): 124
Fat (g): 9.7
Chol (mg): 2.1
Carbo (g): 10.1
Protein (g): 3.8
Calories: 62

4 medium cucumbers, peeled, seeded, and sliced thin

Salt

4 cloves garlic, minced

½ cup plain low-fat yogurt

2 tablespoons nonfat dry milk

Dash freshly ground pepper

¼ cup chopped fresh mint leaves or 2 tablespoons dried mint, crumbled

Place cucumbers in a bowl and sprinkle with salt. Let sit, covered, for 1 hour. Rinse, drain, and pat dry. Mix with garlic, yogurt, and nonfat dry milk. Chill and sprinkle with pepper and mint.

Serves 4

MOZZARELLA MELT

6 cups mixed salad greens such as spinach, radicchio, arugula, curly red lettuce, romaine, and endive leaves

$\frac{1}{2}$ cup Creamy Tofu Dressing or Lemon Sauce (see pgs. 167, 174)

6 ounces part-skim mozzarella cheese

$\frac{1}{4}$ cup wheat germ

1 egg white, beaten

4 teaspoons toasted sesame seeds

Vegetable spray

Dash freshly ground pepper

PER SERVING:
Calcium (mg): 381
Fat (g): 9.6
Chol (mg): 24
Carbo (g): 8.6
Protein (g): 17.1
Calories: 179

Arrange salad greens in attractive composition on individual plates. Spoon dressing over leaves. Slice the mozzarella into thin pieces. Spread wheat germ on a plate or on brown paper. Dip cheese slices into the egg white, then coat with wheat germ, and top with sesame seeds.

Place slices on vegetable-oil-sprayed baking pan and bake in preheated 325°F oven for 5–10 minutes, until cheese is soft but not entirely melted. Transfer with spatula to top of salad and sprinkle with pepper. This is also a fine main course dish served along with sliced ripe tomatoes and a good Italian whole wheat bread.

Serves 4

POTATO SARDINE SALAD

PER SERVING:
Calcium (mg): 269
Fat (g): 6.4
Chol (mg): 58
Carbo (g): 10.2
Protein (g): 12.9
Calories: 149

2 cups sliced cooked new potatoes

$\frac{1}{2}$ cup Bell Peppers Dressing (see pg. 169)

Salt and freshly ground pepper to taste

2 cups fresh mustard greens, chard, or watercress

$\frac{1}{4}$ cup shredded Jarlsberg or Emmenthaler cheese

2 $3\frac{3}{4}$-ounce cans water-packed sardines, including bones, drained

1 tablespoon chopped fresh parsley

In a small bowl, mix the sliced potatoes with Red Pepper Dressing, season with salt and pepper, and chill, covered, for 1 hour. Place the greens on a serving platter and spread the cheese over them; then layer the potatoes and top with the sardines. Garnish with parsley.

Serves 4

RED AND GREEN COLESLAW

1 cup shredded red cabbage

1 cup shredded green cabbage

1 cup chopped celery

1 cup grated raw carrots

1 cup chopped Granny Smith apples

¾ cup plain low-fat yogurt

1 teaspoon fresh lemon juice

2 tablespoons concentrated frozen orange juice

1 teaspoon celery seed

Freshly ground pepper to taste

PER SERVING:
Calcium (mg): 85
Fat (g): 0.6
Chol (mg): 2
Carbo (g): 12.1
Protein (g): 2.5
Calories: 60

Combine cabbages, celery, carrots, and apples in a bowl. Mix together yogurt, lemon juice, orange juice concentrate, and celery seed. Mix dressing with vegetables and allow to chill before serving. Season with fresh pepper to taste.

Serves 6

SARDINES 'N' GREENS

PER SERVING:
Calcium (mg): 238
Fat (g): 5.3
Chol (mg): 68
Carbo (g): 6.9
Protein (g): 12.9
Calories: 216

1 3¾-ounce can water-packed sardines, including bones, drained

3 tablespoons fresh lime juice

1 teaspoon ground cumin

1 teaspoon dried dill weed

Freshly ground pepper to taste

1 tablespoon sliced scallion

2 tablespoons grated raw carrot

2 tablespoons grated raw zucchini or green cabbage

Romaine, escarole, or spinach leaves

1 tablespoon minced fresh parsley

1 tomato, sliced

Mash sardines with a fork. Mix in the lime juice, ground cumin, dill weed, and pepper to taste. Stir in scallions, carrots, and zucchini or cabbage and adjust seasoning. Serve on bed of greens topped with parsley and surrounded by tomato slices. This makes a luncheon salad or appetizer when served with toasted whole wheat pita bread or rice cakes.

Makes 1 cup sardine mixture or 2 servings

SIMPLE SARDINE SALAD

2 cups cauliflower florets

2 cups broccoli florets

2 $3\frac{3}{4}$-ounce cans water-packed sardines, including bones, drained

$\frac{1}{2}$ cup Creamy Garlic Dressing (see pg. 166)

2 tablespoons toasted sesame seeds

PER SERVING:
Calcium (mg): 220
Fat (g): 11.2
Chol (mg): 51
Carbo (g): 8.7
Protein (g): 14.5
Calories: 181

Blanch the cauliflower and broccoli florets and run under cold water. Drain. Place in serving bowl. Break up sardines with a fork and put into bowl with vegetables. Spoon dressing over the sardines and vegetables and toss. Let chill until ready to serve. Sprinkle with sesame seeds.

Serves 4

SNOW PEA SALAD

2 cups snow peas, trimmed

1 cup julienned red bell pepper

$\frac{1}{2}$ cup Creamy Avocado Dressing (see pg. 165)

1 teaspoon toasted sesame seeds

PER SERVING:
Calcium (mg): 39
Fat (g): 1.5
Chol (mg): 0
Carbo (g): 6.7
Protein (g): 21
Calories: 43

Blanch the trimmed snow peas and drain, running under cold water. Pat dry and refrigerate for an hour. When ready to serve, place snow peas in a circle on individual serving plates. Arrange red pepper strips between the pods for a colorful presentation. Spoon dressing over each serving and garnish with sprinkle of sesame seeds.

Serves 4

SPINACH AND NUT SALAD

PER SERVING:
Calcium (mg): 174
Fat (g): 6.3
Chol (mg): 2
Carbo (g): 9.5
Protein (g): 6.2
Calories: 108

1 pound fresh spinach

4 scallions, chopped

1 tablespoon walnut oil

½ cup plain low-fat yogurt

1 tablespoon chopped fresh mint or
    1 teaspoon dried

    Salt and freshly ground pepper to taste

1 clove garlic, minced

2 tablespoons chopped almonds and filberts

Wash spinach leaves well and remove tough stems. Chop fine.
Combine with scallions and place in large nonstick saucepan.
Cook over low heat, stirring until spinach leaves are wilted.
Drain. Add walnut oil and toss. Transfer to serving bowl and
add yogurt, mint, salt and pepper, and garlic. Chill for 2 hours.
Garnish with almonds and filberts.

Serves 4

SPINACH AND ORANGE SALAD

PER SERVING:
Calcium (mg): 83
Fat (g): 0.4
Chol (mg): 0
Carbo (g): 11.9
Protein (g): 2.6
Calories: 55

2 cups raw spinach

2 navel oranges, peeled and sectioned

½ cup thinly sliced red onion

½ cup Lime and Yogurt Sauce (see pg. 175)

Wash spinach leaves well in several changes of water, remove
large stems, and pat dry. Tear into bite-size pieces. Add orange
sections and onion slices. Toss with sauce, chill, and serve.

Serves 4

VEGETABLE COTTAGE CHEESE SALAD

1 cup low-fat cottage cheese

$\frac{1}{4}$ cup chopped fresh parsley

$\frac{1}{4}$ teaspoon salt

Dash freshly ground black pepper

$\frac{1}{4}$ teaspoon toasted sesame seeds

4–6 leaves romaine lettuce, chopped

1 medium ripe tomato, chopped

$\frac{1}{2}$ red or green (or combined) bell pepper, seeded and diced

1 small cucumber, cut into spears (peeled if skin is waxy)

2 thin slices red onion

PER SERVING:
Calcium (mg): 124
Fat (g): 1.7
Chol (mg): 5
Carbo (g): 11
Protein (g): 16.1
Calories: 126

Mix cottage cheese with parsley, salt and pepper, and sesame seeds. Make a bed of chopped romaine and place cottage cheese in its center. Arrange the chopped tomato around the cheese and strew the diced peppers, cucumber spears, and onion around it. Other fresh vegetables may be used as desired.

Serves 2

VEGETABLE SALAD BOWL

PER SERVING:
Calcium (mg): 110
Fat (g): 0.8
Chol (mg): 1
Carbo (g): 15.4
Protein (g): 5.1
Calories: 84

2 cups escarole and chicory

2 ripe tomatoes, sliced

$\frac{1}{2}$ cup blanched green beans

$\frac{1}{2}$ cup cooked lima beans or kidney beans, rinsed and drained if canned

$\frac{1}{2}$ cucumber, peeled and sliced

1 cup sliced zucchini

$\frac{1}{4}$ cup sliced mushrooms

1 cup broccoli florets

2 carrots, cut into julienne strips

$\frac{1}{2}$ cup sliced radishes

1 red onion, sliced thin

1 cup Buttermilk Mustard Dressing (see pg. 164)

Wash and trim the escarole and chicory and pat or spin dry. Arrange on salad plates and place vegetables over the greens. Spoon Buttermilk Mustard Dressing over each salad.

Serves 6

WATERCRESS EGG SALAD

2 bunches watercress, trimmed of tough ends, washed, and dried

2 hard-cooked egg whites

2 tablespoons coarsely chopped red onion

4 tablespoons Glorious Green Dressing (see pg. 168)

1 tablespoon toasted pumpkin seeds or sesame seeds

PER SERVING:
Calcium (mg): 67
Fat (g): 3.1
Chol (mg): 1
Carbo (g): 4.8
Protein (g): 5.2
Calories: 63

Toss watercress, egg whites, and onion with dressing until coated. Serve on individual salad plates with topping of seeds.

Serves 4

ZUCCHINI SALAD

1 ½ pounds zucchini

1 cup plain low-fat yogurt

1 teaspoon fresh lemon juice

1 tablespoon chopped fresh dill

1 tablespoon minced fresh parsley

2 scallions, sliced

½ teaspoon crystalline fructose

Salt and freshly ground pepper to taste

Few dashes paprika

PER SERVING:
Calcium (mg): 94
Fat (g): 0.6
Chol (mg): 2
Carbo (g): 6
Protein (g): 3
Calories: 40

Wash zucchini and slice into thin rounds. Mix well remaining ingredients except paprika and then blend thoroughly with sliced zucchini. Sprinkle top with few dashes of paprika. Chill for a few hours before serving.

Serves 6

CHAPTER 7 **SALAD DRESSINGS**

Dressings are a matter of individual taste. What's sauce for a salad may also be sauce for dessert. Only one dressing in this chapter is oil-based, and that one is intended especially for greens and uses balsamic vinegar. Most of the other milk- or yogurt-based recipes may be used on salad, over vegetables, or with broiled or baked meats, fish, or poultry. Since the milk is universal, many of them double as dessert toppings. For further fun in dressing up any variety of dishes, turn back to the appetizer section and thin out some of these spreads or dips with more milk or even a drop of water. Also refer to Chapter 8, where you'll find sauces that can also be used on salads.

ALMOND GINGER SAUCE

PER SERVING:
Calcium (mg): 18
Fat (g): 1.2
Chol (mg): 0
Carbo (g): 1.3
Protein (g): 0.8
Calories: 18

¼ cup toasted almonds, skins removed

¾ cup buttermilk

1 teaspoon grated fresh ginger

½ teaspoon low-sodium soy sauce

Dash salt

2 teaspoons concentrated frozen orange juice

Place almonds in food processor or blender and chop. Add remaining ingredients and blend. Place in saucepan and bring to simmer. Remove from heat. Serve warm over vegetables, fish, or grains or chill and serve over berries or fresh fruit.

Makes 1 cup or 16 1-tablespoon servings

ANCHOVY YOGURT DRESSING

PER SERVING:
Calcium (mg): 23
Fat (g): 1.6
Chol (mg): 1
Carbo (g): 1
Protein (g): 0.7
Calories: 21

1 cup plain low-fat yogurt

2 tablespoons safflower or corn oil

¼ cup white wine vinegar

Pinch salt

¼ teaspoon white pepper

1 clove garlic, minced

¼ cup chopped fresh parsley

2 tablespoons anchovies, rinsed

Cayenne pepper

Place all ingredients in a blender and process until smooth. Refrigerate to develop taste. Adjust seasoning before serving. Excellent dressing for vegetables, pasta, fish, salads.

Makes about 1¼ cups or 20, 1-tablespoon servings

BALSAMIC VINAIGRETTE

1 tablespoon Dijon mustard
$\frac{1}{4}$ cup balsamic vinegar (available in specialty food shops)
2 tablespoons water
2 tablespoons fresh lemon juice
$\frac{1}{4}$ teaspoon dried tarragon
1 clove garlic, minced fine
Salt and freshly ground pepper to taste
$\frac{1}{4}$ cup safflower oil

PER SERVING:
Calcium (mg): 1
Fat (g): 3.9
Chol (mg): 0
Carbo (g): 0.4
Protein (g): 0.1
Calories: 37

In a jar, combine the mustard, vinegar, water, lemon juice, tarragon, garlic, and salt and pepper. Shake well to combine. Pour in oil and shake again. Chill before serving.

Makes about $\frac{3}{4}$ cup or 12, 1-tablespoon servings

BLUE CHEESE DRESSING

$\frac{1}{4}$ cup crumbled blue cheese
$\frac{1}{2}$ cup plain low-fat yogurt
$\frac{1}{2}$ cup buttermilk
$\frac{1}{2}$ clove garlic, minced
2 dashes cayenne pepper
Dash freshly ground black pepper
$\frac{1}{2}$ teaspoon dried oregano

PER SERVING:
Calcium (mg): 21
Fat (g): 0.5
Chol (mg): 1
Carbo (g): 0.7
Protein (g): 0.7
Calories: 9

Blend all ingredients together and refrigerate.

Makes about $1\frac{1}{2}$ cups or 24, 1-tablespoon servings

BUTTERMILK MUSTARD DRESSING

PER SERVING:
Calcium (mg): 22
Fat (g): 0.2
Chol (mg): 1
Carbo (g): 1
Protein (g): 0.6
Calories: 9

$\frac{1}{2}$ cup buttermilk

$\frac{1}{4}$ cup plain low-fat yogurt

2 teaspoons Dijon mustard

$1\frac{1}{2}$ tablespoons peeled, seeded, and grated cucumber

1 tablespoon finely chopped green onion

2 teaspoons chopped fresh parsley

1 teaspoon each grated lemon zest and orange zest

Dash white pepper

Blend all ingredients together and chill before serving.

Makes about 1 cup or 16, 1-tablespoon servings

CREAMY AVOCADO DRESSING

1 ripe avocado

3 tablespoons fresh lemon juice

$\frac{1}{4}$ cup chopped onion

2 tablespoons seeded and chopped
jalapeño pepper

$\frac{1}{2}$ cup plain low-fat yogurt

$\frac{1}{4}$ cup evaporated skim milk

Salt and freshly ground black pepper
to taste

PER SERVING:
Calcium (mg): 10
Fat (g): 1
Chol (mg): 0
Carbo (g): 1.2
Protein (g): 6
Calories: 14

Scoop pulp out of avocado and place in blender or food processor container. Add lemon juice, onion, and jalapeño pepper. Process to blend. Add yogurt and evaporated milk and process until smooth. Add salt and pepper to taste.

Makes 2 cups or 32, 1-tablespoon servings

CREAMY GARLIC DRESSING

$\frac{1}{2}$ cup evaporated skim milk

2 tablespoons strained fresh lemon juice

2 large cloves garlic, minced

$\frac{1}{4}$ teaspoon salt

1 teaspoon dried dill weed

1 teaspoon concentrated frozen apple juice

$\frac{1}{4}$ teaspoon paprika

$\frac{1}{4}$ teaspoon white pepper

2 dashes sesame oil (available in oriental section of supermarket)

Dash cayenne pepper

Whip all ingredients together in blender until smooth. Chill before serving. Adjust seasoning. Good as salad dressing or topping for tofu.

Makes about $\frac{3}{4}$ cup or 12, 1-tablespoon servings

CREAMY TOFU DRESSING

1 cup soft tofu (bean curd)
1 large clove garlic, sliced
2 tablespoons low-sodium soy sauce
Juice of 1 lemon with pulp
$\frac{1}{4}$ teaspoon dried oregano
$\frac{1}{4}$ teaspoon dried marjoram
3 tablespoons balsamic vinegar
2 tablespoons chopped scallion
$\frac{1}{4}$ cup water (or as needed)

PER SERVING:
Calcium (mg): 11
Fat (g): 0.3
Chol (mg): 0
Carbo (g): 0.7
Protein (g): 0.7
Calories: 8

Place tofu in food processor or blender with remaining ingredients, adding only as much water as needed to make desired consistency.

Makes 2 cups or 32, 1-tablespoon servings

GLORIOUS GREEN DRESSING

1/4 cup chopped fresh parsley

1/4 cup chopped fresh kale, spinach, or chard

1 tablespoon chopped fresh dill weed or
1 teaspoon dried dill

1 cup plain low-fat yogurt

Dash cayenne pepper

Salt and freshly ground black pepper
to taste

Blend all ingredients quickly in food processor. Adjust seasoning. Chill before serving.

Variation: Dilute with buttermilk for thinner dressing.

Makes about 1 1/2 cups or 24, 1-tablespoon servings

HORSERADISH DRESSING-SPREAD

1/4 cup plain low-fat yogurt

1/4 cup low-fat cottage cheese, rinsed in cold
water and drained

1 teaspoon prepared horseradish (sugarless)

1/4 teaspoon minced garlic

Dash cayenne pepper

Puree all ingredients together in blender. Nice with fish, on sardines or salads, and as an appetizer.

Makes about 1/2 cup or 8, 1-tablespoon servings

BELL PEPPERS DRESSING

½ red bell pepper, cored, seeded, and chopped (about ½ cup)

½ fresh tomato, diced (about ¼ cup)

2 chopped fresh basil leaves or ½ teaspoon dried basil

2 tablespoons chopped onions

Dash dried thyme

Dash cayenne pepper

½ teaspoon dried tarragon

Salt and freshly ground black pepper to taste

2 teaspoons balsamic vinegar

1 teaspoon walnut oil

½ cup buttermilk

PER SERVING:
Calcium (mg): 7
Fat (g): 0.2
Chol (mg): 0
Carbo (g): 0.6
Protein (g): 0.3
Calories: 5

In a food processor or blender, puree red bell pepper, tomato, basil, onion, thyme, cayenne, tarragon, and salt and pepper with vinegar and oil. Add buttermilk and stir together. Chill before serving. Delicious served over salads, vegetables, pasta, or broiled fish.

Makes about 1½ cups or 24, 1-tablespoon servings

RUSSIAN DRESSING

PER SERVING:
Calcium (mg): 8
Fat (g): 0.1
Chol (mg): 1
Carbo (g): 0.6
Protein (g): 1.3
Calories: 9

1 cup low-fat cottage cheese, rinsed in cold water and drained

2 tablespoons plain low-fat yogurt

1 tablespoon fresh lemon juice

1/4 cup tomato juice

1 tablespoon chopped gherkins

1 hard-cooked egg white, chopped

Salt and freshly ground pepper to taste

Quickly puree cottage cheese, yogurt, and lemon juice in a blender, then add the tomato juice. Stir in the gherkins and egg white by hand and season with salt and pepper. Refrigerate before serving.

Makes about 1 1/4 cups or 20, 1-tablespoon servings

TOMATO VELOUTÉ

PER SERVING:
Calcium (mg): 6
Fat (g): 0
Chol (mg): 0
Carbo (g): 0.8
Protein (g): 0.4
Calories: 5

1/2 cup evaporated skim milk

1/4 teaspoon Dijon mustard

1/4 teaspoon salt

Freshly ground pepper

2 tablespoons tarragon vinegar

2 tablespoons fresh lemon juice

1/4 cup tomato juice

1 tablespoon minced fresh parsley

Chill the milk. Combine mustard, salt, pepper, vinegar, and lemon juice. Stir the tomato juice into the chilled milk, then add the vinegar-lemon mixture gradually, stirring until blended. Add parsley, adjust seasoning, and blend well.

Makes 1 cup or 16, 1-tablespoon servings

WATERCRESS DRESSING

1 cup watercress leaves, well washed

½ cup part-skim ricotta cheese

⅔ cup buttermilk

1 tablespoon nonfat dry milk

3 tablespoons chopped scallion

1 tablespoon anchovy paste

1 teaspoon white wine vinegar

1 teaspoon fresh lemon juice

¼ teaspoon dried tarragon, crushed

    Salt and freshly ground pepper to taste

PER SERVING:
Calcium (mg): 19
Fat (g): 0.4
Chol (mg): 1
Carbo (g): 0.7
Protein (g): 0.7
Calories: 9

In a food processor, chop the watercress leaves, then add remaining ingredients and blend. Chill and serve over vegetables.

Makes 2 cups or 32, 1-tablespoon servings

YOGURT "MAYONNAISE" FINES HERBES

6 tablespoons plain low-fat yogurt

2 tablespoons (or less) tarragon vinegar

2 tablespoons low-sodium soy sauce

1 tablespoon chopped herbs, such as fresh basil, parsley, dill, oregano

½ teaspoon chopped onion

1 sliver garlic, minced

½ teaspoon Dijon mustard

Salt and freshly ground pepper

Mix all ingredients together well and chill before serving to blend flavors. Excellent dressing for coleslaw, vegetables, broiled fish or meat.

Variation: For a thinner dressing, add buttermilk as desired.

Makes ¾ cup or 12, 1-tablespoon servings

CHAPTER 8 **SAUCES**

Yogurt, buttermilk, evaporated skim milk, nonfat dry milk, and tofu may be used as bases for original and imaginative sauces. Add fruit, seeds or nuts, carob, coffee, molasses, or juice or make your own combinations. These add flair and flavor to desserts and baked goods, and some may even be used as salad dressings, according to individual taste. They all add calcium in a tasteful way.

Goat's milk, kefir, and soy milk may be substituted, for those with a lactose intolerance or merely for a change of taste.

CURRY SAUCE

PER SERVING:
Calcium (mg): 29
Fat (g): 0.8
Chol (mg): 1
Carbo (g): 2.1
Protein (g): 0.9
Calories (g): 19

1 teaspoon corn oil

1 onion, minced

1–2 teaspoons curry powder

1/2 cup plain low-fat yogurt

1/2 teaspoon salt

In nonstick skillet, heat oil and cook onion. Stir in curry powder and add yogurt and salt. Simmer for about 2 minutes, stirring. Serve over vegetables, fish, or chicken.

Makes 1/2 cup or 8, 1-tablespoon servings

LEMON SAUCE

PER SERVING:
Calcium (mg): 29
Fat (g): 0.8
Chol (mg): 1
Carbo (g): 2.1
Protein (g): 0.9
Calories (g): 19

1 lemon, washed, unpeeled, cut into pieces

2 dashes sesame oil

1 cup soft tofu (bean curd)

1/2 cup buttermilk

1/2 teaspoon prepared horseradish

1 teaspoon Dijon mustard

1/4 teaspoon salt

Freshly ground pepper to taste

1 tablespoon chopped black olives (optional)

Place lemon pieces in blender or food processor with the oil and blend until lemon is chopped into small pieces. Add remaining ingredients and blend until smooth. Chill and serve as dip for fresh vegetables or as dressing for artichokes, fish, or even grains.

Makes 2 cups or 32, 1-tablespoon servings

LIME AND YOGURT SAUCE

2 tablespoons fresh lime juice
2 tablespoons water
1 teaspoon salt
Dash freshly ground pepper
1/4 cup plain low-fat yogurt

PER SERVING:
Calcium (mg): 13
Fat (g): 0.3
Chol (mg): 0.1
Carbo (g): 0.7
Protein (g): 0.4
Calories (g): 5

Stir together first 4 ingredients. Add yogurt and blend. Delicious over fresh fruit.

Makes 1/2 cup or 8, 1-tablespoon servings

MANGO CHEESE SAUCE

1 mango, pulp pureed to make 1 cup
1/2 cup part-skim ricotta cheese
1/4 cup low-fat cottage cheese
1 teaspoon fresh lemon juice

PER SERVING:
Calcium (mg): 13
Fat (g): 0.3
Chol (mg): 1
Carbo (g): 1.5
Protein (g): 0.8
Calories (g): 12

Blend all ingredients until smooth in a food processor. Serve over fresh fruit or baked goods. Also tasty over some salads. Makes a great sauce for a banana split or peach melba.

Makes about 2 cups or 32, 1-tablespoon servings

MISSISSIPPI MUD SAUCE

PER SERVING:
Calcium (mg): 19
Fat (g): 2.5
Chol (mg): 0
Carbo (g): 4.1
Protein (g): 1.9
Calories (g): 39

1/4 cup carob powder

1 tablespoon crystalline fructose

1/2 cup evaporated skim milk

1/4 cup chunky peanut butter

1/4 teaspoon pure vanilla extract

In a small saucepan, stir together the carob, fructose, and milk and bring to simmer. Remove from heat, beat in peanut butter with a wire whisk, and add vanilla. Stir until combined. This gets slightly thicker as it chills. Use as sauce for fruits, cream desserts, or even a bread such as Orange Ginger Bread (see pg. 189).

Makes about 1/2 cup or 8, 1-tablespoon servings

PAPAYA PUREE

PER SERVING:
Calcium (mg): 12
Fat (g): 0
Chol (mg): 0
Carbo (g): 2.4
Protein (g): 0.4
Calories (g): 11

1 ripe papaya

1/4 cup evaporated skim milk

2 tablespoons nonfat dry milk

Dash white pepper

1/8 teaspoon pure vanilla extract

1/4 teaspoon grated fresh ginger

Peel papaya and scoop out pulp. Save seeds for garnish. Place papaya pulp in blender or food processor and puree. Add remaining ingredients. This is a multipurpose sauce! If using to sauce chicken, fish, or veal, heat before serving. Chill if using as a dessert sauce over fruit.

Makes 1 cup or 16, 1-tablespoon servings

POPEYE PESTO

1 pound fresh spinach, well rinsed, tough stems trimmed

½ cup plain low-fat yogurt

½ cup low-fat cottage cheese

¼ cup grated Parmesan cheese

2 tablespoons dried basil

¼ cup chopped almonds

2 cloves garlic

¼ cup chopped fresh parsley, stems removed

PER SERVING:
Calcium (mg): 38
Fat (g): 0.9
Chol (mg): 1
Carbo (g): 1.5
Protein (g): 1.6
Calories (g): 19

Steam spinach lightly in just the water remaining on leaves. Drain. Combine all ingredients in food processor or blender and blend until smooth. Serve over pasta, warm or chilled.

Makes about 2 cups or 32, 1-tablespoon servings

POPPY SEED SAUCE

1 cup plain low-fat yogurt

2 teaspoons grated orange zest

1 teaspoon grated lemon zest

2 tablespoons raspberry or apple cider vinegar

1 tablespoon concentrated frozen orange juice

3 tablespoons poppy seeds

PER SERVING:
Calcium (mg): 40
Fat (g): 0.8
Chol (mg): 1
Carbo (g): 1.5
Protein (g): 0.9
Calories (g): 16

Stir all ingredients together until well blended. Refrigerate for several hours to develop taste. Refreshing served over fresh fruit or fruit salads.

Makes about 1¼ cups or 20, 1-tablespoon servings

RICOTTA PEANUT BUTTER

PER SERVING:
Calcium (mg): 26
Fat (g): 2.6
Chol (mg): 2
Carbo (g): 1.6
Protein (g): 2.1
Calories (g): 37

1/4 cup chunky peanut butter

1/2 cup evaporated skim milk

1/2 cup part-skim ricotta cheese

1 teaspoon ground cinnamon

2 teaspoons concentrated frozen orange juice

1 teaspoon toasted sesame seeds

Mix all ingredients together, stirring well to blend. Refrigerate before serving. Use as topping for potatoes or casseroles, over noodles or rice, or as a snack or appetizer.

Makes 1 cup or 16, 1-tablespoon servings

SAUCY ORANGE CHIFFON

PER SERVING:
Calcium (mg): 21
Fat (g): 0.4
Chol (mg): 2
Carbo (g): 2.4
Protein (g): 1
Calories (g): 17

1/2 cup evaporated skim milk

3 ounces part-skim ricotta cheese

1/4 cup concentrated frozen orange juice

1 tablespoon chopped fresh mint or 1/2 teaspoon dried mint, crushed

Place all ingredients in a blender and process until smooth. Chill before serving. Delicious over fruit or baked goods. Topped with cut chives, parsley, or basil, it is also tasty served over turkey, veal, chicken, fish, and salads or vegetables.

Makes about 1 cup or 16, 1-tablespoon servings

VIENNA CREAM SAUCE

½ cup plain low-fat yogurt
½ cup part-skim ricotta cheese
1½ tablespoons blackstrap molasses
3 tablespoons chopped hazelnuts and almonds
2 tablespoons chopped dried figs

PER SERVING:
Calcium (mg): 31
Fat (g): 1.1
Chol (mg): 2
Carbo (g): 2.6
Protein (g): 1.1
Calories (g): 23

Mix the yogurt and ricotta together until smooth. Add the remaining ingredients and chill until ready to serve. Spoon over fresh fruits. It is particularly piquant served over sliced bananas as a split! Also something special over baked treats.

Makes about 1½ cups or 24, 1-tablespoon servings

YOGURT FRUIT SAUCE

½ cup plain Yogurt Sour Cream
(see note below)
4 teaspoons sugar-free fruit conserve

PER SERVING:
Calcium (mg): 35
Fat (g): 0.3
Chol (mg): 1
Carbo (g): 2.1
Protein (g): 1
Calories (g): 15

Stir together yogurt and fruit conserve and chill 30 minutes or more. Delightful topping for fruits, cakes, or crackers.

Note: To make ½ cup plain Yogurt Sour Cream, follow recipe for Yogurt Sour Cream (see pg. 254), using 1 cup plain nonfat or low-fat yogurt.

Makes about ¾ cup or 12, 1-tablespoon servings

CHAPTER 9 **BREADS AND MUFFINS**

Baked goods are a prime way to provide calcium. Most folks have their own favorite breads, puddings, soufflés, and baked desserts. By adding more nonfat dry milk or substituting skim milk, buttermilk, or evaporated skim milk for whole milk products and cheese, you can give your recipes a substantial calcium boost. Baking may also be done with kefir, soy milk, and goat's milk for those who cannot digest lactose. The addition of raisins, chopped figs or dates, sesame seeds, sunflower or pumpkin seeds, almonds, and filberts gives more flavor and crunch, and more calcium, too.

Some of these recipes may double as dessert, served with a creamy dessert sauce, and some as a main course. Whether the goodies are mini muffins or soufflés, high-calcium baking is a boon!

BOSTON BROWN BREAD

〰〰〰〰〰〰〰〰〰〰〰〰〰〰〰

PER SLICE:
Calcium (mg): 49
Fat (g): 2
Chol (mg): 20
Carbo (g): 15.3
Protein (g): 2.7
Calories (g): 87

½ cup whole wheat flour
½ cup all-purpose unbleached flour
¼ cup cornmeal
1 tablespoon wheat germ
½ teaspoon baking powder
¼ teaspoon baking soda
¼ teaspoon salt
1 egg, beaten
1 cup blackstrap molasses
1 tablespoon crystalline fructose
2 tablespoons nonfat dry milk
2 teaspoons safflower oil
¾ cup buttermilk
2 tablespoons sunflower seeds
3 tablespoons raisins
Vegetable spray

Stir together flours, cornmeal, wheat germ, baking powder, baking soda, and salt. In another bowl, combine egg, molasses, fructose, dry milk, and oil. Add the flour mixture to the liquid, alternating with additions of the buttermilk. Beat together well. Stir in sunflower seeds and raisins. Coat 2, 16-ounce empty cans with cooking spray and turn batter into them in equal portions. Cover tightly with foil and place in a large Dutch oven. Pour boiling water into the pot to a depth of 1 inch and bring back to a boil. Reduce heat, cover, and simmer over low heat for about 3 hours, until bread tests done (when toothpick inserted in center comes out clean). Add more water to the pot if needed. Lift cans out and let stand 10 minutes on a wire rack before removing breads. Serve warm with Crème Fraîche or Whipped Ricotta Cream (see pgs. 250, 253).

Makes 2 loaves, each about 7 slices

BUTTERMILK SODA BREAD

1 cup whole wheat flour

1 cup plus 1 tablespoon all-purpose unbleached flour

1/4 cup wheat germ

2 tablespoons crystalline fructose

2 teaspoons baking soda

2 teaspoons double-acting baking powder

1/2 teaspoon salt

2 cups buttermilk

1 1/2 tablespoons safflower oil

2 tablespoons toasted sunflower seeds

2 tablespoons chopped dried figs

Vegetable spray

PER SERVING:
Calcium (mg): 54
Fat (g): 2.4
Chol (mg): 1
Carbo (g): 16
Protein (g): 3.4
Calories (g): 97

Stir all dry ingredients together in large bowl, then add buttermilk and oil until batter is blended but still lumpy. Add sunflower seeds and chopped figs and mix. Coat a 9-inch round pan with vegetable oil spray and dust with extra all-purpose flour. Spoon batter into the pan and bake in preheated 375°F oven for 50–60 minutes, until a toothpick inserted in the center comes out clean. Cool bread for 10 minutes in pan, then turn out on wire rack. Cut into wedges to serve.

Makes about 16 servings

CAROB-NUT BREAD PUDDING

PER SERVING:
Calcium (mg): 165
Fat (g): 3.8
Chol (mg): 37.4
Carbo (g): 17.1
Protein (g): 7.1
Calories (g): 120

1/4 cup unsweetened carob powder

6 tablespoons water

3 cups skim milk

3 tablespoons concentrated frozen orange juice

1/8 teaspoon salt

2 eggs (1 yolk only)

2 tablespoons part-skim ricotta cheese

1/2 teaspoon ground cinnamon

Vegetable spray

4 slices day-old or toasted whole wheat bread, processed to rough cubes in blender (the better the bread, the better the pudding!)

1/4 cup chopped almonds and hazelnuts

Sift carob powder into a mixing bowl and stir in the water until smooth. Add milk, orange juice concentrate, salt, eggs, ricotta, and cinnamon and blend together in blender or food processor.

Coat two 4 by 8-inch loaf pans with vegetable oil spray and line with bread crumbs. Over this pour the carob mixture, stir, and let stand about 20 minutes to absorb the liquid. Stir. Top with nuts.

Preheat oven to 350°F and place the loaf pans in another pan containing 1 inch of hot water. Bake for 50–60 minutes or until a toothpick inserted in the middle comes out clean.

Serves 8–10

CHILI-CHEESE CORNBREAD

1 ¼ cups yellow or blue cornmeal

2 teaspoons baking powder

½ teaspoon baking soda

½ teaspoon salt

¼ cup whole wheat flour

1 ¼ cups buttermilk

2 eggs (1 yolk only), beaten lightly

¼ cup shredded sharp Cheddar cheese or Formagg

2 tablespoons chopped mild green chilies (more or less as desired)

Vegetable spray

PER SERVING:
Calcium (mg): 54
Fat (g): 1.5
Chol (mg): 23
Carbo (g): 12.5
Protein (g): 3.2
Calories (g): 76

Sift together into a large bowl 1 cup plus 2 tablespoons of cornmeal and the baking powder, soda, salt, and flour. Stir in the buttermilk, eggs, cheese, and chilies, combining well.

Coat an 8-inch square baking pan with vegetable oil spray and sprinkle it with remaining 2 tablespoons of cornmeal. Turn the batter into the pan and bake in upper third of preheated 450°F oven for 10 minutes or until it is firm in center.

Makes about 12, 2-inch servings

COTTAGE OAT BREAD

1 1/2 cups whole wheat flour

2 tablespoons active dry yeast

3 tablespoons minced onion

1/2 cup hot water

2 cups low-fat cottage cheese

2 tablespoons walnut oil

1/2 cup nonfat dry milk

1 teaspoon salt

2 tablespoons crystalline fructose

2 eggs (1 yolk only)

1 cup quick-cooking or rolled oats

2 tablespoons dill seeds or fennel

2 teaspoons caraway seeds

1 1/2 cups all-purpose unbleached flour

Vegetable spray

Place the whole wheat flour and yeast in large bowl of an electric mixer. In food processor or blender, combine the onion, water, cottage cheese, walnut oil, dry milk, salt, fructose, and eggs. Process until smooth. Turn into the bowl of flour and beat for 2 minutes. Then stir in the oats, seeds, and unbleached flour.

Coat a large bowl with vegetable oil spray and turn the mixture into it. Cover and let rise in a warm place for about an hour or until doubled in bulk. Punch down, place in a greased 1 1/2-quart casserole, and let rise, uncovered, for 45 minutes or until again twice its bulk. In the meantime, preheat oven to 350°F. Bake 1 hour or until the loaf sounds hollow when tapped.

Makes 1 large loaf, 12–14 slices

GREEN AND RED CABBAGE BREAD

Vegetable spray
1 teaspoon fresh lemon juice
1/2 cup finely shredded red cabbage
1/2 cup finely shredded green cabbage
1/2 cup plain low-fat yogurt
1 egg
1/4 cup concentrated frozen orange juice
1/4 cup nonfat dry milk
1/4 cup safflower oil
1 cup whole wheat flour
3/4 cup all-purpose unbleached flour
1/4 cup toasted sesame seeds
2 teaspoons baking powder
1/2 teaspoon baking soda
1/8 teaspoon ground mace
1/8 teaspoon ground ginger

PER SERVING:
Calcium (mg): 75
Fat (g): 8.3
Chol (mg): 28
Carbo (g): 20.5
Protein (g): 5.4
Calories (g): 174

Preheat oven to 350°F. Coat a loaf pan with vegetable oil spray. Mix lemon juice with red and green cabbage and set aside. Mix yogurt with egg, orange juice concentrate, dry milk, and oil, blending well. Then add cabbage. In a separate bowl, mix the remaining dry ingredients together thoroughly. Gradually pour the wet mixture into the dry and mix to blend. Pour into loaf pan and bake 35–45 minutes, until browned and tester comes out clean when inserted in middle of loaf. Remove and let cool on rack.

Serves 10

NORWEGIAN NUT BREAD

PER SLICE:
Calcium (mg): 65
Fat (g): 5
Chol (mg): 24
Carbo (g): 22.7
Protein (g): 5.9
Calories (g): 151

1 cup sifted all-purpose unbleached flour

1 teaspoon baking soda

1 teaspoon salt

½ cup chopped almonds, filberts, and sunflower seeds

¼ cup nonfat dry milk

1 cup unsifted whole wheat flour

½ cup raisins

1 tablespoon grated orange zest

1 beaten egg

1 cup buttermilk

1 tablespoon walnut oil

Vegetable spray

Preheat oven to 375°F. Measure sifted flour into a mixing bowl with baking soda and salt. Add nuts, dry milk, whole wheat flour, and raisins. Combine orange zest, egg, buttermilk, and walnut oil and stir into the flour mixture until well blended.

Coat 2, 16-ounce empty cans with vegetable oil spray and spoon mixture into them. Bake for 50 minutes or until golden. Loosen around edges with a spatula and turn onto rack to cool. Serve with Low-Fat Cream Cheese or Make-Believe Mayo (see pg. 251).

Makes 2 small loaves, about 6 slices each

ORANGE GINGER BREAD

1 package active dry yeast

$1/2$ cup warm water or warmed yogurt whey (see pg. 240)

$1/4$ teaspoon ground ginger

$1/2$ teaspoon crystalline fructose

3 tablespoons concentrated frozen orange juice

1 teaspoon caraway seeds

1 teaspoon salt

2 tablespoons grated orange zest

2 tablespoons walnut oil

12 ounces evaporated skim milk

1 cup rye flour

Freshly ground pepper

2 cups all-purpose unbleached flour

$1/2$ cup nonfat dry milk

Vegetable spray

PER WEDGE:
Calcium (mg): 82
Fat (g): 2.6
Chol (mg): 0
Carbo (g): 30
Protein (g): 5.7
Calories (g): 167

In a large mixing bowl, dissolve yeast in warm water or whey. Blend in ginger and fructose. Let stand until yeast foams, about 5 minutes. Add orange juice concentrate, caraway seeds, salt, orange zest, oil, and evaporated skim milk. Add the rye flour and black pepper and mix until batter is smooth. Gradually add the all-purpose flour and nonfat dry milk, mixing until smooth and satiny.

Turn into 2 vegetable-oil-sprayed casseroles (about 1 quart each) and let rise, covered, in a warm place until dough doubles or fills the dishes. Bake in preheated 350°F oven for 50–60 minutes or until a toothpick inserted into the center comes out clean. Let cool a few minutes, then remove and cool on rack.

Makes 2 loaves, about 12 wedges each

SESAME BREAD

1 cup low-fat cottage cheese

1 package active dry yeast

$\frac{1}{4}$ cup warm water

1 tablespoon crystalline fructose

$\frac{1}{4}$ teaspoon baking soda

1 egg, beaten

4 tablespoons toasted sesame seeds

$\frac{1}{4}$ cup nonfat dry milk

1 teaspoon salt

1 scant cup whole wheat flour

1 scant cup all-purpose unbleached flour

2 tablespoons wheat germ

Vegetable spray

Heat the cottage cheese until just warm. Soften the yeast in the warm water. After 5 minutes, add the yeast mixture to the cottage cheese, then add the fructose, baking soda, egg, sesame seeds, nonfat dry milk, and salt and mix well. Turn into a bowl.

Combine the flours and wheat germ and gradually add to the cottage cheese mixture, stirring to blend. Cover and let stand in a warm place for a few hours, until doubled in bulk. Stir down to original size and turn into a vegetable-oil-sprayed loaf pan. Cover with a cloth and again let stand to double for about an hour.

Bake in preheated 350°F oven for 40 minutes. Loaf is done when it sounds hollow when tapped. Let cool in refrigerator before slicing. Nice when toasted, too.

Makes 1 loaf, about 16–18 slices

CHEDDAR BREAD

1 package active dry yeast

¼ cup warm water or yogurt whey (see pg. 240)

½ teaspoon crystalline fructose

1 tablespoon safflower oil

¾ cup skim milk

2 tablespoons nonfat dry milk

½ cup plain low-fat yogurt

¼ cup grated sharp Cheddar cheese or low-fat Formagg cheese substitute

1 teaspoon salt

1 cup all-purpose unbleached flour

2 cups whole wheat flour

Vegetable spray

1 tablespoon dill seed

1 tablespoon toasted sesame seeds

PER SLICE:
Calcium (mg): 54
Fat (g): 2.2
Chol (mg): 3
Carbo (g): 17.6
Protein (g): 4.3
Calories (g): 105

Dissolve yeast in warm water or whey with fructose. Stir in the oil, milks, yogurt, cheese, and salt. Add the all-purpose flour, beating to blend, and then gradually stir in the whole wheat flour until dough is stiff. Turn onto a floured board and knead for 5 minutes. Add more whole wheat flour if necessary (oil hands for this task as it is a sloppy one!).

Place dough in a bowl coated with vegetable oil spray, turning to coat the dough. Cover and let rise in a warm place until doubled in size. Punch down and form into a loaf. Put into a 4 by 8-inch loaf pan also coated with cooking spray. Cover and let rise until doubled in bulk, about 1 hour. Sprinkle top of loaf with seeds. Bake in preheated 375°F oven for 50 minutes.

Makes 1 loaf, about 16 slices

PARMESAN GOURMET MUFFINS

PER MUFFIN:
Calcium (mg): 54
Fat (g): 2.4
Chol (mg): 1
Carbo (g): 16
Protein (g): 3.4
Calories (g): 97

1 cup buttermilk

1 egg

1 1/2 tablespoons walnut oil

1 cup all-purpose unbleached flour

1/4 cup whole wheat flour

1 teaspoon baking powder

1/2 teaspoon baking soda

1/4 teaspoon salt

6 tablespoons grated Parmesan or sapsago cheese

1/2 teaspoon dried rosemary, crushed

Vegetable spray

Beat together the buttermilk, egg, and oil. In a large bowl sift together the flours, baking powder, baking soda, and salt. Combine grated cheese and rosemary in a separate dish. Add 4 tablespoons of the grated cheese mixture to the dry ingredients and toss with a fork to blend. Pour the buttermilk mixture into the center of the flour and combine with fork until blended but still lumpy.

Coat 2 mini-muffin tins with vegetable oil spray and spoon the mixture into the cups, filling any empty ones with water. Top each muffin cup with sprinkling of remaining cheese and rosemary mixture. Place pans in upper third of preheated 350°F oven for 20–25 minutes until toothpick inserted in center of muffins comes out clean. Muffins should be nicely browned.

Makes 20 mini-muffins

CORNMEAL MUFFINS

Vegetable spray
1 cup cornmeal
1 cup whole wheat pastry flour
1 tablespoon poppy seeds
1 tablespoon baking powder
½ cup nonfat dry milk
1 cup water
2 egg whites
2 tablespoons walnut oil
1 tablespoon crystalline fructose
½ cup raisins
12 almonds

PER MUFFIN:
Calcium (mg): 92
Fat (g): 5
Chol (mg): 1
Carbo (g): 24
Protein (g): 5.5
Calories (g): 155

Coat muffin tin with spray and preheat oven to 400°F. Combine cornmeal, flour, poppy seeds, and baking powder. In a smaller bowl mix together the dry milk, water, egg whites, walnut oil, and fructose. Turn into the dry mixture and blend well. Stir the raisins into the batter and spoon into muffin tins. Top each muffin with one almond. Bake for 40 minutes until golden.

Makes 12 large muffins

OAT BRAN MUFFINS

PER MUFFIN:
Calcium (mg): 30
Fat (g): 2.4
Chol (mg): 16
Carbo (g): 7.8
Protein (g): 2.8
Calories (g): 51

Vegetable spray

2 1/4 cups oat bran cereal

2 tablespoons crystalline fructose

1/4 cup chopped almonds

2 tablespoons chopped dried figs

1 teaspoon baking powder

1/2 teaspoon salt

1/4 cup concentrated frozen orange Juice

3/4 cup buttermilk

1 egg

1 egg white

2 tablespoons vegetable oil

Coat muffin tin with vegetable oil spray or line with paper baking cups. Combine all dry ingredients. Add remaining ingredients and mix together well. Fill muffin tins about three-fourths full and bake in preheated 425°F oven for about 15 minutes, until golden.

Makes 18 muffins

PARMESAN POPOVERS

Vegetable spray

4 egg whites at room temperature

1/3 cup plus 2 tablespoons nonfat dry milk

1 cup water

3/4 cup all-purpose unbleached flour

1/4 cup whole wheat flour

2 tablespoons Best Butter (see pg. 249)

1/8 teaspoon freshly grated nutmeg

6 teaspoons grated Parmesan or
sapsago cheese

PER SMALL MUFFIN:

Calcium (mg): 43
Fat (g): 4.8
Chol (mg): 4
Carbo (g): 8.7
Protein (g): 3.3
Calories (g): 70

PER LARGE MUFFIN:

Calcium (mg): 86
Fat (g): 4.8
Chol (mg): 8
Carbo (g): 17.4
Protein (g): 6.6
Calories (g): 140

Preheat oven to 450°F and coat a 12-cup muffin tin or 6 custard cups with vegetable oil spray. Place all ingredients except the cheese in blender or food processor and blend for 15–20 seconds, being careful not to overmix. Pour batter into the muffin tin or custard cups. Sprinkle each muffin top with ½ teaspoon of the grated cheese or use 1 teaspoon on each custard cup.

Bake batter in the muffin tin for 15 minutes or in the custard cups for 20 minutes. Reduce heat to 350°F and bake each for the same amount of time at the lower heat. Remove and serve at once.

Makes 12 small or 6 large muffins

CHAPTER 10 **DESSERTS**

Ice cream is usually the prescription for women who need extra calcium. But the eggs and sugar and heavy cream that make up this rich dessert negate its benefits. The "ice creams" found in this chapter are more truly ice milks or sherbets. They are easily made of skim milk, yogurt, or buttermilk with fruits, carob, cocoa, nuts, and spices. A simple ice cream maker or just a metal ice tray and a blender or food processor are the only tools needed.

Some low-fat custards and mousses are also included on the following pages, as are a few delicious cream pies. Throughout the year you can enjoy desserts using summer berries by simply freezing them (or buying frozen) and storing them for later use. Combine berries or any fruit with low-fat yogurt, kefir, part-skim ricotta, or any of the recipes in the chapters on sauces or basics that appeal to you. Buttermilk is a wonderful base for a cold fruit soup, so popular in Scandinavia. The Perfect Pie Crust or Graham Cracker Crust (see pgs. 252, 250) may be filled with myriad choices for calcium-rich delicious desserts.

ALMOND APPLE ICE CREAM

PER SERVING:
Calcium (mg): 74
Fat (g): 2.4
Chol (mg): 1
Carbo (g): 16
Protein (g): 3.4
Calories (g): 97

1 apple, cored and diced

1 frozen banana

1 envelope nonfat dry milk

1 cup water

1 tablespoon concentrated frozen orange juice

½ teaspoon pure vanilla extract

1 teaspoon instant regular or decaf coffee

1 tablespoon slivered blanched almonds

Dash freshly grated nutmeg

Blend all ingredients except last 2 in food processor. Pour into metal tray and place in freezer, stirring periodically and processing again before serving. Top with almonds and a dash of nutmeg.

Serves 4

BANANA MAPLE ICE CREAM

1 cup evaporated skim milk

2 cups sliced frozen bananas

$\frac{1}{2}$ teaspoon imitation maple flavoring

2 tablespoons chopped hazelnuts and almonds

PER SERVING:
Calcium (mg): 54
Fat (g): 2.4
Chol (mg): 1
Carbo (g): 16
Protein (g): 3.4
Calories (g): 97

Pour evaporated milk into metal tray and place in freezer for about an hour. Slice frozen bananas, place in food processor with the frozen milk, and blend until smooth and creamy. Add maple flavoring and blend again. Return to metal tray and stir in the nuts. Cover with foil and replace in freezer. Take out to stir with a fork from time to time before serving. This is best served at once or not more than 1 hour after refreezing.

Serves 4

BANANA TOFU ICE CREAM

6 ounces tofu (bean curd)

2 medium frozen bananas, sliced

4 ice cubes, crushed or shaved

1 teaspoon crystalline fructose

1 teaspoon blackstrap molasses

1/4 teaspoon freshly grated nutmeg

1/4 cup nonfat dry milk

1/2 cup water

1/2 teaspoon pure vanilla extract (or more to taste)

1 tablespoon chopped almonds and hazelnuts

Place all ingredients except nuts in food processor and blend until smooth. Place in bowl in freezer for a short time and then transfer to refrigerator before serving. This is a pudding-like cream and may even be eaten immediately following preparation. Do not let it freeze hard. Sprinkle a few chopped nuts over each serving.

Serves 4

FUDGE FREEZE

1 cup skim milk
1 egg
3 egg whites
1 teaspoon pure vanilla extract
1/4 cup carob powder
2 tablespoons nonfat dry milk
1 teaspoon instant regular or decaf coffee
2 teaspoons crystalline fructose
    Dash salt
1 tablespoon roughly chopped hazelnuts

PER SERVING:
Calcium (mg): 231
Fat (g): 2.5
Chol (mg): 70
Carbo (g): 11.1
Protein (g): 5.8
Calories (g): 81

Heat the milk in a small saucepan to scald and remove from heat. Place remaining ingredients except hazelnuts in a blender. Cover and process on slow, then remove cover and pour in hot milk. Process again for about a minute. Turn into metal tray and place in freezer, stirring periodically to break up ice crystals. Stir in hazelnuts before serving.

Serves 4

ORANGE MIST

PER SERVING:
Calcium (mg): 82
Fat (g): 20
Chol (mg): 0
Carbo (g): 13.9
Protein (g): 5
Calories (g): 78

1 cup freshly squeezed orange juice

2 teaspoons fresh lemon juice

1 teaspoon grated orange zest

1 cup evaporated skim milk

Mix together orange and lemon juices and orange zest. Pour into metal tray and place in freezer for 1–2 hours, stirring periodically.

Pour the milk into a small metal bowl and put in freezer along with the beaters of an electric mixer. Remove milk after an hour, when crystals have begun to form. Quickly beat until the milk is whipped into stiff peaks.

Remove orange freeze and beat separately for a minute. Then fold into the whipped milk and return to freezer for 30–45 minutes before serving in sherbet glasses. Do not make this too far ahead.

Serves 4

PAPAYA PISTACHIO CREAM

1 ripe papaya, peeled and seeded (reserve some seeds for garnish)

1 cup plain low-fat yogurt

½ teaspoon pure vanilla extract

1 teaspoon fresh lime juice

1 teaspoon grated orange zest

Ground cinnamon

2 tablespoons peeled and chopped pistachios

PER SERVING:
Calcium (mg): 127
Fat (g): 2.9
Chol (mg): 4
Carbo (g): 12.5
Protein (g): 4.2
Calories (g): 88

Place papaya pulp in food processor and puree with yogurt. Add vanilla, lime juice, and orange zest. Pour into metal tray and place in freezer, stirring frequently. Do not leave in freezer longer than 1–2 hours. Spoon out onto dessert dishes and garnish with cinnamon and nuts, plus papaya seeds if desired. May be served immediately rather than frozen.

Serves 4

PEACH FREEZE

2 cups peeled, pitted, and mashed fresh peaches

1 cup plain low-fat or nonfat yogurt

1 teaspoon pure vanilla extract

2 tablespoons unflavored gelatin

2 tablespoons concentrated frozen orange juice

1 tablespoon grated orange zest

Toasted sesame seeds

Ground cinnamon

Combine peaches, yogurt, and vanilla until well mixed. Sprinkle the gelatin over the orange juice concentrate and wait 5 minutes before dissolving the gel over hot water. Then combine with peach mixture.

Place in metal tray, cover, and put in freezer for about 1 hour, stirring periodically. Do not allow this to freeze solid. Before serving, stir again, spoon into 4 dessert glasses, and top with grated orange zest, sesame seeds, and cinnamon.

Serves 4

PINEAPPLE GINGER FROGURT

1 cup plain low-fat yogurt

½ cup crushed canned unsweetened pineapple

1 teaspoon grated fresh ginger

½ banana

1 teaspoon crystalline fructose

½ teaspoon pure vanilla extract

1 tablespoon sunflower seeds

PER SERVING:
Calcium (mg): 112
Fat (g): 2
Chol (mg): 4
Carbo (g): 15.5
Protein (g): 3.8
Calories (g): 91

Combine all ingredients except sunflower seeds and blend in a food processor until smooth. Turn into metal tray and place in freezer. After 30 minutes or so, scrape sides and stir to break up crystals. Repeat. Do not leave in the freezer longer than two hours before serving. May also be prepared in ice cream maker. Sprinkle with sunflower seeds before serving.

Serves 4

CANTALOUPE SHERBET

PER SERVING:
Calcium (mg): 149
Fat (g): 0.3
Chol (mg): 2
Carbo (g): 14
Protein (g): 4.7
Calories (g): 75

3 cups peeled, seeded, and cubed cantaloupe

1 cup nonfat dry milk

2 tablespoons concentrated frozen orange juice

2 cups water

$\frac{1}{4}$ teaspoon freshly grated nutmeg

1 teaspoon pure vanilla extract

$\frac{1}{2}$ teaspoon ground cinnamon

2 tablespoons fresh lemon juice

Place cantaloupe in food processor and puree. Add remaining ingredients and process until blended. Turn into metal trays and put in freezer, stirring every so often to break up crystals. Process again before serving. May be used as dessert, served with sliced fruits, or on waffles or ladyfingers.

Serves 6

ICED MOCHA SHERBET

1 1/2 cups evaporated skim milk

1 teaspoon pure vanilla extract

2 tablespoons carob powder

1 tablespoon crystalline fructose

2 tablespoons concentrated frozen orange juice

1 tablespoon instant regular or decaf coffee

1 tablespoon part-skim ricotta cheese

PER SERVING:
Calcium (mg): 121
Fat (g): 0.5
Chol (mg): 1
Carbo (g): 27.2
Protein (g): 7.1
Calories (g): 101

Mix all ingredients together in blender and turn into metal tray. Place in freezer and stir with fork from time to time to break up ice crystals. When ready to serve, process again so that sherbet is soft.

Serves 4

PURPLE SHERBET

1 cup chopped, seeded MacIntosh apple

1 cup natural grape juice

1/2 cup nonfat dry milk

1/2 teaspoon pure vanilla extract

PER SERVING:
Calcium (mg): 75
Fat (g): 0.2
Chol (mg): 1
Carbo (g): 12.8
Protein (g): 2.3
Calories (g): 60

Place all ingredients in blender or food processor and puree until frothy. Pour into metal tray and place in freezer, stirring often to break up ice crystals. Process again before serving.

Serves 6

COFFEE CUSTARD CUPS

PER SERVING:
Calcium (mg): 47
Fat (g): 1.4
Chol (mg): 66
Carbo (g): 8.9
Protein (g): 7.1
Calories (g): 80

2 eggs (1 yolk only)

1 cup evaporated skim milk

1 teaspoon instant regular or decaf coffee

½ teaspoon pure vanilla extract

1 tablespoon concentrated frozen orange juice

1 tablespoon grated orange zest

Ground cinnamon

Process eggs in blender, then add evaporated milk, instant coffee, vanilla, and orange juice concentrate. Pour into 4 individual custard cups and place in a larger baking pan filled with about 1 inch of boiling water. Bake in preheated 350°F oven for 45 minutes or until a knife inserted in the center comes out clean. Remove from oven, chill, run a knife around edges of cups, invert, and garnish each custard with sprinkling of orange zest and cinnamon.

Serves 4

PEANUT CUSTARD

2 tablespoons peanut butter

1 cup evaporated skim milk, divided

2 eggs (1 yolk only)

½ teaspoon pure vanilla extract

4 teaspoons chopped roasted peanuts

PER SERVING:
Calcium (mg): 91
Fat (g): 7.2
Chol (mg): 69
Carbo (g): 9.4
Protein (g): 10
Calories (g): 142

Stir together the peanut butter and ½ cup of the milk in a small bowl. In a separate bowl, whisk the eggs and add the remaining milk, then the peanut butter mixture and vanilla. Turn into a small ovenproof baking dish or into 4 individual custard cups and place in a larger pan containing about an inch of boiling water. Bake in preheated 350°F oven for about 45 minutes or until a knife inserted in the center comes out clean. Cool, turn out onto dessert dishes, and serve garnished with peanuts.

Serves 4

ALMOND DELIGHT

2 teaspoons walnut oil

½ cup blanched almonds

⅓ cup semolina grain

1½ cups skim milk

2 tablespoons nonfat dry milk

3 teaspoons crystalline fructose

½ teaspoon pure vanilla extract

2 tablespoons chopped dried figs, plumped in water

Heat walnut oil in large nonstick skillet. Sauté almonds for 2–3 minutes. Add semolina grain and cook, stirring, until lightly browned. In a small saucepan, bring skim milk, dry milk, and fructose to a boil. Pout this into the semolina and almond mixture and stir. Let simmer a few minutes, until thick. Add vanilla extract and drained figs, stir, and serve warm in dessert dishes.

Serves 4

CAROB CREAM

1 teaspoon unflavored gelatin
$1/4$ cup cold water
4 tablespoons carob powder
Pinch salt
1 cup evaporated skim milk, divided
1 egg yolk, beaten
$1/2$ teaspoon pure vanilla extract
2 tablespoons chopped almonds and hazelnuts

PER SERVING:
Calcium (mg): 120
Fat (g): 3.6
Chol (mg): 68
Carbo (g): 14.3
Protein (g): 7.9
Calories (g): 108

Sprinkle gelatin over cold water until firm. Then place over a bowl of hot water to dissolve. In a saucepan, combine carob powder, salt, the dissolved gelatin, and half of the milk and mix until blended. Add egg yolk and stir together over low heat until thick. Stir in vanilla extract with wire whisk. Remove from heat and let cool.

In the meantime, pour remaining milk into a metal bowl and place in freezer for an hour, until crystals form around edges. Also place the beaters of an electric mixer in freezer to chill. When cold enough, beat until stiff. Then fold the carob mixture into the whipped milk and beat together until peaks form.

Serve at once in sherbet dishes or place in freezer for 30 minutes before serving. This does not hold and needs to be made close to mealtime. It might also be served with a scattering of fruit. Top with nuts before serving.

Serves 4

APRICOT MOUSSE

PER SERVING:
Calcium (mg): 136
Fat (g): 2.6
Chol (mg): 0
Carbo (g): 12.8
Protein (g): 9.8
Calories (g): 106

$\frac{1}{2}$ cup dried apricots, dried prunes, or a combination

$\frac{1}{2}$ cup soft tofu (bean curd)

2 teaspoons pure vanilla extract

2 tablespoons nonfat dry milk

2 egg whites at room temperature

Fresh mint leaves (optional)

Soak fruits in hot water for 30 minutes, then drain. Drain the soft tofu between paper towels and turn into the container of a food processor or blender along with the fruit, vanilla, and dry milk. Process. Whip the egg whites until stiff but not dry. Pour fruit mixture into a bowl and fold egg whites into it. Spoon into dessert glasses, garnish with mint, and serve chilled.

Makes about 1 cup or 2, $\frac{1}{2}$-cup servings

MANGO MOUSSE

PER SERVING:
Calcium (mg): 92
Fat (g): 0.6
Chol (mg): 0
Carbo (g): 29.3
Protein (g): 5.6
Calories (g): 137

2 ripe mangoes or papaya (2 cups pulp)

1 cup hulled and rinsed fresh strawberries

$\frac{1}{2}$ teaspoon pure vanilla extract

$1\frac{1}{2}$ cups evaporated skim milk

1 tablespoon concentrated frozen orange juice

Puree all ingredients in food processor or blender and pour into metal trays. Place in freezer and stir every 30 minutes or so to break up ice crystals. Blend again before serving.

Makes 4 cups or 6, $\frac{2}{3}$-cup servings

BANANA BERRY RICE PUDDING

1 cup cooked brown rice

½ cup mashed banana

½ cup nonfat dry milk

¾ cup water

1 teaspoon maple extract

1 teaspoon ground cinnamon

1 teaspoon toasted sesame seeds

¼ cup concentrated frozen orange juice

2 tablespoons fresh blueberries or
   1 tablespoon raisins

2 egg whites, beaten stiff

1 tablespoon sunflower seeds

PER SERVING:
Calcium (mg): 92
Fat (g): 0.6
Chol (mg): 0
Carbo (g): 29.3
Protein (g): 5.6
Calories (g): 137

Mix together all ingredients except egg whites and sunflower seeds. Fold egg whites into rice mixture and pour into 4-inch by 8-inch baking pan. Top with sprinkling of sunflower seeds. Bake in preheated 350°F oven for 1 hour or until pudding is set.

Serves 6

BANANA SWEET POTATO PUDDING

1/2 pound sweet potatoes, peeled and cubed (about 1 cup)

1 cup water

2 medium bananas, sliced

1 cup skim milk

2 tablespoons nonfat dry milk

1/2 teaspoon coconut extract

1 small cinnamon stick

1 tablespoon concentrated frozen orange juice

1/2 teaspoon pure vanilla extract

2 tablespoons slivered almonds

Boil the sweet potatoes in water for 20 minutes or until tender. Drain off any excess water and add bananas, milk, coconut extract, cinnamon stick, and orange juice concentrate. Cook about 15 minutes or until thick. Remove cinnamon stick and add vanilla. Puree in blender or food processor and serve either warm or chilled, topped with slivered almonds.

Serves 6

COFFEE CREAM PUDDING

1 envelope unflavored gelatin

¼ cup concentrated frozen orange juice

1 cup strong freshly brewed regular or decaf coffee

1 tablespoon crystalline fructose

1 cup low-fat cottage cheese

¼ cup part-skim ricotta cheese

1 egg, separated

4 tablespoons sugar-free fruit conserve (raspberry, peach, or any flavor desired)

12 almonds and filberts

PER SERVING:
Calcium (mg): 78
Fat (g): 3.3
Chol (mg): 76
Carbo (g): 13.9
Protein (g): 12.3
Calories (g): 132

In a small bowl, sprinkle the gelatin on the concentrated orange juice. Add coffee and fructose. Stir to dissolve gelatin. Place cottage cheese and ricotta in food processor container, drop in egg yolk, and process. Add gelatin mixture and repeat. Pour into metal tray and place in freezer for no more than 30 minutes, so that it does not freeze.

In the meantime, whip the egg white until it is stiff. Remove cottage cheese mixture from freezer and fold in egg white. Turn into individual molds or 1, 3-cup ring mold. Into the center of each portion place ½ tablespoon of the fruit conserve. Refrigerate until set.

When ready to serve, unmold by dipping in hot water for a second or loosening with a sharp knife. Top with remaining fruit conserve and nuts. May also be served with orange slices or other fresh fruit.

Serves 4

BERRIES AND YOGURT À L'ORANGE

PER SERVING:
Calcium (mg): 118
Fat (g): 1.5
Chol (mg): 3.5
Carbo (g): 19.5
Protein (g): 3.9
Calories (g): 99

1 cup plain low-fat yogurt

$\frac{1}{8}$ teaspoon freshly grated nutmeg

$\frac{1}{8}$ teaspoon ground mace

$\frac{1}{2}$ teaspoon finely chopped orange zest

1 pint strawberries, halved or sliced

1 pint blackberries or blueberries

4 twists of orange peel

Mix yogurt with the spices and chopped orange zest. Chill. Wash and trim the berries. Divide berries among 4 parfait glasses or dessert dishes and top with the yogurt sauce. Garnish each with orange twist.

Note: Any fruit may be substituted, such as peaches, bananas, plums, nectarines, orange segments, kiwi fruit, melon, etc.

Serves 4

MEDITERRANEAN MELON

½ teaspoon ground cinnamon (or more to taste)

1 cup plain Yogurt Sour Cream (see note below)

2 cups peeled, seeded, and cubed honeydew melon or cantaloupe

2 tablespoons chopped almonds and filberts

Mint sprigs

PER SERVING:
Calcium (mg): 224
Fat (g): 4.1
Chol (mg): 7
Carbo (g): 14.4
Protein (g): 7.3
Calories (g): 118

Stir cinnamon into the yogurt and adjust to taste. Mix the melon with the yogurt and nuts and serve chilled in dessert glasses with a sprig of mint as garnish.

Note: To make 1 cup plain Yogurt Sour Cream, follow recipe for Yogurt Sour Cream (see pg. 254), using 2 cups plain low-fat or nonfat yogurt.

Serves 4

PEACH MELBA

4 large ripe peaches

1 cup plus 2 tablespoons raspberries

½ cup part-skim ricotta cheese

2 tablespoons nonfat dry milk

2 tablespoons water

1 tablespoon grape juice

PER SERVING:
Calcium (mg): 120
Fat (g): 2.7
Chol (mg): 10
Carbo (g): 16.5
Protein (g): 5.1
Calories (g): 104

Blanch peaches by dropping them into boiling water for 30 seconds. Remove, run under cold water, and peel off skins. Cut in half, discard pits, and place 2 peach halves on each of 4 individual dessert dishes. Puree raspberries with remaining ingredients, reserving 2 tablespoons of berries for garnish. Spoon puree over peaches, top with berries, and serve cold.

Serves 4

RASPBERRY PARFAIT

PER SERVING:
Calcium (mg): 119
Fat (g): 2.3
Chol (mg): 4
Carbo (g): 9.8
Protein (g): 6
Calories (g): 77

1 envelope unflavored gelatin

$\frac{1}{4}$ cup cold water

10 ounces frozen unsweetened raspberries, thawed

1 cup plain low-fat yogurt

$\frac{1}{2}$ teaspoon pure vanilla extract

2 egg whites at room temperature

1 teaspoon crystalline fructose

1 tablespoon slivered blanched almonds

In a mixing bowl, soften the gelatin in cold water and then place over hot water to dissolve. Stir in the raspberries, yogurt, and vanilla and chill. In the meantime, beat egg whites until frothy and add the fructose. Beat again until peaks form, then fold into the raspberry mixture. Chill until set. Serve in parfait glasses, topped with slivered almonds.

Serves 4

RED, WHITE, AND BLUE BAKE

12 ounces farmer cheese

¼ cup pineapple juice (or more as needed)

½ teaspoon salt (or more to taste)

6 rings canned unsweetened pineapple slices

¾ cup fresh blueberries

½ cup sliced fresh strawberries

Vegetable spray

1 tablespoon toasted sunflower seeds

Pinch ground cinnamon

1 cup Saucy Orange Chiffon (see pg. 178)

PER SERVING:
Calcium (mg): 71
Fat (g): 1.1
Chol (mg): 2
Carbo (g): 13.7
Protein (g): 6.8
Calories (g): 90

Crumble farmer cheese and mix with pineapple juice and salt. Cube the pineapple rings, keeping 2 whole for garnish. Reserve some berries for garnish and mix remainder into cheese. Spray 4 by 8-inch loaf pan and turn cheese and fruit mixture into it. Pat down firmly and top with extra berries, pineapple, sunflower seeds, and cinnamon.

Bake in preheated 350°F oven for 20 minutes. Remove, let cool for 30 minutes, and chill in refrigerator for 1 ½ hours. Cut around edges with a spatula and transfer loaf to serving dish. Slice and serve with other fruits or crisp crackers, if desired, and Saucy Orange Chiffon.

Note: Other combinations of fruit may be used, such as peaches, bananas, plums, and raisins.

Serves 8

RUSSIAN RHUBARB

1 pound rhubarb, washed and trimmed
1/4 cup concentrated frozen orange juice
2 tablespoons water
2 tablespoons crystalline fructose
1 cup sliced strawberries
Crème Fraîche (see pg. 250)

Soak rhubarb in cold water for 10 minutes. Drain, slice into chunks, and place in saucepan with orange juice concentrate, 2 tablespoons water, and fructose. Simmer, covered, for 10–15 minutes, until soft and stringy. Add strawberries, stir, chill, and serve with dollop of Crème Fraîche.

Serves 4

STUFFED FIGS

12 large dried figs, split horizontally
24 blanched almonds
1/4 cup Crème Fraîche or Saucy Orange Chiffon (see pgs. 250, 178)

Soak figs in hot water to soften for about 30 minutes. Drain and pat dry. Stuff each fig with 2 almonds and pinch closed. Arrange on cookie sheet and bake in preheated 325°F oven for 10 minutes. Remove and serve at room temperature with a dollop of Crème Fraîche or Saucy Orange Chiffon.

Serves 12

FRUIT DELIGHT

2 teaspoons unflavored gelatin

3 tablespoons canned unsweetened pineapple juice

2 cups low-fat cottage cheese

4 tablespoons nonfat dry milk

½ orange, peeled, de-seeded, and diced

½ cup sliced strawberries

½ cup blueberries

½ cup Grape-Nuts

2 tablespoons sunflower seeds

PER SERVING:
Calcium (mg): 72
Fat (g): 1.8
Chol (mg): 3
Carbo (g): 11.8
Protein (g): 9.1
Calories (g): 98

Soften gelatin in pineapple juice and after 5 minutes heat over hot water to dissolve. Mix together with cottage cheese and nonfat dry milk in a blender or food processor.

In the meantime, arrange the fruit in an attractive pattern in bottom of an 8-inch metal mold. Pour the cottage cheese mixture over the fruit, cover, and refrigerate for a few hours.

When ready to serve, immerse mold in a little warm water to loosen. Turn upside down onto a serving dish and garnish with Grape-Nuts and sunflower seeds.

Serves 8

CAROB CREAM PIE

PER SERVING:
Calcium (mg): 194
Fat (g): 8.6
Chol (mg): 13
Carbo (g): 11
Protein (g): 7.4
Calories (g): 148

1 baked Graham Cracker Crust (see pg. 250)

1 cup part-skim ricotta cheese

1 cup plain Yogurt Sour Cream (see note below)

2 teaspoons carob or cocoa powder

$1/2$ teaspoon pure vanilla extract

6 hazelnuts

6 almonds

Dash ground cinnamon

Fresh berries (optional)

Bake crust as directed and let cool. Place ricotta and yogurt in a large bowl with carob powder and vanilla and beat together with electric mixer until smoothly blended. Turn into the baked pie shell, decorate the top with an arrangement of the nuts, and refrigerate until firm. Top with dusting of cinnamon and a fresh berry or two if available.

Note: To make 1 cup plain Yogurt Sour Cream, follow recipe for Yogurt Sour Cream (see pg. 254), using 2 cups plain nonfat or low-fat yogurt.

Serves 8

KIWI LIME PIE

1 cup plain Yogurt Sour Cream
(see note below)

1 cup part-skim ricotta cheese

2 tablespoons crystalline fructose

1 teaspoon concentrated frozen orange juice

½ teaspoon pure vanilla extract

Juice of two limes

1 baked Graham Cracker Crust (see pg. 250)

2 kiwi fruits, peeled and sliced into thin
rounds (or use thinly sliced oranges)

PER SERVING:
Calcium (mg): 197
Fat (g): 7.5
Chol (mg): 13
Carbo (g): 16.2
Protein (g): 7.4
Calories (g): 157

Place yogurt in mixing bowl with ricotta cheese, fructose, orange juice concentrate, vanilla, and lime juice. Beat with electric mixer until creamy. Pour into pie shell and chill until set. Before serving, arrange fruit slices so that they overlap each other in a decorative pattern.

Note: To make 1 cup plain Yogurt Sour Cream, follow recipe for Yogurt Sour Cream (see pg. 254), using 2 cups plain nonfat or low-fat yogurt.

Serves 8

MOCHA FILLING

PER SERVING:
Calcium (mg): 160
Fat (g): 4.8
Chol (mg): 13
Carbo (g): 14.4
Protein (g): 5.4
Calories (g): 101

1 cup part-skim ricotta cheese

1 teaspoon ground cinnamon

1 1/2 teaspoons carob powder

2 tablespoons crystalline fructose

1/2 teaspoon pure vanilla extract

2 tablespoons chopped almonds

Blend all ingredients except almonds in food processor and add a little skim milk for desired consistency, if necessary. Pour into serving bowl. Top with almonds when served over ladyfingers, graham crackers, or in pie made with Perfect Pie Crust (see pg. 252).

Serves 6

RICOTTA RAISIN TARTS

1/2 cup raisins

1/4 cup port wine

1 cup part-skim ricotta cheese

1 tablespoon grape juice

2 teaspoons grated lemon zest

Pinch salt

1/2 teaspoon pure vanilla extract

1/4 cup chopped almonds and hazelnuts

1 recipe Perfect Pie Crust dough (see pg. 252)

Plump raisins in wine for about 2 hours and then pour into a small saucepan and cook until liquid has evaporated. Mix cheese with the grape juice, lemon zest, salt, and vanilla. Stir in the cooled raisins and nuts.

Meanwhile, make the dough, roll thin, and cut into 8 rounds (use a cup or a glass); shape to fit 8-cup muffin tin. Bake in preheated 350°F oven for 20–30 minutes, until brown. Remove from oven and let cool. These shells may be made ahead and kept in the freezer.

Stuff tarts with ricotta mixture and return to oven for 10 minutes. Let cool, remove from muffin tin, and serve.

Serves 8

CHAPTER 11 **BEVERAGES**

Some soft drinks now have added calcium, but the caffeine and other chemicals and additives also in these drinks negate any benefits. The drinks you can make at home are infinite in their variety, from the simplest "egg cream" of seltzer, skim milk, and coffee to Hot Russians and cinnamon cocoa or a health drink of yogurt, blackstrap molasses, and wheat germ. Goat's milk, kefir, and soy milk—even CalciMilk for the lactose intolerant—will combine in a shake. Buttermilk, yogurt, tofu, frozen bananas, berries, orange juice, skim milk, and combinations of some dessert sherbets blended with ice cubes will yield smooth and nourishing beverages with punch. Many of these shakes are delicious breakfast alternatives blended with your favorite cereal, bran, or wheat germ. Others serve as a great snack or relaxing bedtime beverage.

Simple mineral waters are laden with calcium: Mountain Valley, produced in California, contains a hefty 380 mg of calcium per liter! The Italian San Pellegrino water has more than 200 mg per liter, Ferrarelle 446 mg per liter, and French Contrexeville has 451 mg per liter. If your tap water is hard, chances are it is high in calcium, too. Cheers!

ALMOND CAROB MILK SHAKE

PER SERVING:
Calcium (mg): 214
Fat (g): 4.7
Chol (mg): 2.1
Carbo (g): 118
Protein (g): 6.6
Calories (g): 106

$\frac{1}{4}$ cup blanched almonds

2 tablespoons carob powder

2 cups skim milk

2 tablespoons nonfat dry milk

$\frac{1}{4}$ teaspoon pure vanilla extract

4 tablespoons crushed ice

Process almonds in blender until they are ground fine. Add remaining ingredients and blend until frothy.

Serves 4

EGGNOG

PER SERVING:
Calcium (mg): 438
Fat (g): 0.4
Chol (mg): 6
Carbo (g): 18
Protein (g): 13.9
Calories (g): 134

1 egg white

1 $\frac{1}{2}$ cups skim milk

$\frac{1}{2}$ cup nonfat dry milk

$\frac{1}{2}$ teaspoon crystalline fructose

$\frac{1}{2}$ teaspoon pure vanilla extract

4 ice cubes, crushed

$\frac{1}{4}$ teaspoon freshly grated nutmeg

Blend all ingredients except nutmeg at high speed for 30 seconds. Garnish with dusting of nutmeg.

Serves 4

FIZZY STRAWBERRY FREEZE

1 cup frozen unsweetened strawberries
1 cup skim milk
2 tablespoons nonfat dry milk
½ teaspoon crystalline fructose
½ cup cold seltzer

PER SERVING:
Calcium (mg): 212
Fat (g): 0.5
Chol (mg): 3
Carbo (g): 13.3
Protein (g): 6.1
Calories (g): 80

Puree all ingredients except the seltzer in a blender. Pour into 2 tall glasses and add half the seltzer to each glass for a frothy fruit drink.

Serves 2

FRAN'S FRAPPE

1 cup buttermilk
¼ cup nonfat dry milk
½ cup fresh blueberries or strawberries
½ teaspoon fructose
4 ice cubes, crushed
  Extra berries

PER SERVING:
Calcium (mg): 250
Fat (g): 1.3
Chol (mg): 6
Carbo (g): 15.4
Protein (g): 7.3
Calories (g): 100

Blend all ingredients together and pour into 2 tall glasses. Garnish each with a whole strawberry or a few blueberries.

Serves 2

FROZEN BANANA SHAKE

PER SERVING:
Calcium (mg): 192
Fat (g): 0.5
Chol (mg): 2.5
Carbo (g): 17.5
Protein (g): 5.7
Calories (g): 87

1 frozen banana

2 tablespoons carob powder

2 tablespoons nonfat dry milk

2 cups skim milk

1 tablespoon wheat germ

4 ice cubes, crushed

Cut frozen banana into chunks. Place all ingredients in blender or food processor and blend until smooth.

Serves 4

HAPPY HEALTH SHAKE

PER SERVING:
Calcium (mg): 287
Fat (g): 1.9
Chol (mg): 7
Carbo (g): 14.6
Protein (g): 6.8
Calories (g): 100

1 cup plain low-fat yogurt

1 tablespoon blackstrap molasses

2 teaspoons wheat germ

Whip all ingredients together in a blender and pour into 2 tall, frosted glasses.

Serves 2

MELON MIXER

1 cup cubed cantaloupe or honeydew melon
½ cup plain low-fat yogurt
½ cup skim milk
½ teaspoon freshly grated nutmeg
1 tablespoon concentrated frozen
  orange juice
Mint sprig
Small wedge lemon

PER SERVING:
Calcium (mg):
  187.5
Fat (g): 0.5
Chol (mg): 5
Carbo (g): 20.5
Protein (g): 10.2
Calories (g): 115

Blend together all ingredients except mint and lemon, which should be used for garnish.

Serves 2

MOCHA MILK SHAKE

1 tablespoon instant regular or decaf coffee
2 tablespoons carob powder
2 tablespoons nonfat dry milk
2 cups skim milk
4 ice cubes, crushed

PER SERVING:
Calcium (mg): 381
Fat (g): 0.5
Chol (mg): 5
Carbo (g): 20.5
Protein (g): 10.2
Calories (g): 115

Place all ingredients in blender or food processor and mix until frothy. Pour into 2 chilled glasses.

Serves 2

ORANGE BRACER

PER SERVING:
Calcium (mg): 89
Fat (g): 0.2
Chol (mg): 1
Carbo (g): 16.6
Protein (g): 4.6
Calories (g): 86

1 cup freshly squeezed orange juice

1 egg white

$\frac{1}{2}$ cup nonfat dry milk

$\frac{1}{2}$ teaspoon pure vanilla extract

2 ice cubes, crushed

2 orange slices

Blend all ingredients, except orange slices, at high speed and serve in frosted glasses, garnished with orange slices.

Serves 2

PEACHY SLIM NOG

PER SERVING:
Calcium (mg): 260
Fat (g): 0.4
Chol (mg): 3
Carbo (g): 27.2
Protein (g): 7.7
Calories (g): 139

$\frac{1}{2}$ cup skim milk

2 tablespoons nonfat dry milk

1 cup sliced fresh peaches

1 tablespoon concentrated frozen apple juice

$\frac{1}{4}$ teaspoon freshly grated nutmeg

Blend all ingredients except nutmeg until smooth and frothy. Garnish with dusting of nutmeg.

Serves 1

PINEAPPLE-BANANA SHAKE

1 cup fresh pineapple chunks
1 frozen banana, sliced
1/2 cup plain low-fat yogurt
1/2 cup skim milk
1 egg white
4 ice cubes, crushed
4 fresh pineapple wedges

PER SERVING:
Calcium (mg): 101
Fat (g): 0.7
Chol (mg): 2.5
Carbo (g): 20.1
Protein (g): 3.9
Calories (g): 96

Blend all ingredients except pineapple wedges until smooth and frothy. Pour into 4 frosted glasses and garnish each with pineapple wedge.

Serves 4

PURPLE COW

1 cup buttermilk
1/2 cup grape juice
1/4 teaspoon pure vanilla extract

PER SERVING:
Calcium (mg): 198
Fat (g): 1.1
Chol (mg): 4.5
Carbo (g): 15
Protein (g): 4.4
Calories (g): 88

Blend ingredients together for 30 seconds until frothy and pour into 2 frosted glasses.

Serves 2

TOFU SHAKE

PER SERVING:
Calcium (mg): 143
Fat (g): 1.9
Chol (mg): 1.5
Carbo (g): 14.7
Protein (g): 6.2
Calories (g): 95

3 ounces soft tofu (bean curd)
1 medium frozen banana, sliced
1 cup skim milk
2 tablespoons wheat germ
4 ice cubes, crushed
    Dash freshly grated nutmeg
    Dash ground cinnamon

Blend all but last 2 ingredients together in a food processor or blender and serve with sprinkling of nutmeg and cinnamon.

Serves 2

TOMATO SHAKE

PER SERVING:
Calcium (mg): 172
Fat (g): 1.4
Chol (mg): 5
Carbo (g): 12.5
Protein (g): 5.8
Calories (g): 82

1 cup tomato juice or V-8
¾ cup plain low-fat yogurt
1 tablespoon fresh lemon juice
    Dash celery salt
2 small stalks celery with leaves

Blend together all ingredients except celery stalks. Pour into 2 tall glasses and garnish with celery stalks.

Serves 2

CINNAMON HOT "CHOCOLATE"

2 cups skim milk

2 tablespoons nonfat dry milk

1 tablespoon carob powder

½ teaspoon pure vanilla extract

2 cinnamon sticks

PER SERVING:
Calcium (mg): 367
Fat (g): 0.5
Chol (mg): 5
Carbo (g): 108
Protein (g): 10
Calories (g): 108

In a saucepan, combine the first 3 ingredients and bring to a simmer. Remove from heat and add vanilla, stirring in well. Pour into 2 cups and garnish each with a cinnamon stick.

Serves 2

HOT RUSSIANS

1 tablespoon instant regular or decaf coffee

1 tablespoon frozen concentrated orange juice

3 tablespoons hot water

2 cups skim milk

2 tablespoons nonfat dry milk

½ teaspoon pure vanilla extract

1 teaspoon grated orange zest

½ teaspoon ground cinnamon

PER SERVING:
Calcium (mg): 178
Fat (g): 0.2
Chol (mg): 2
Carbo (g): 8.7
Protein (g): 5
Calories (g): 57

Combine instant coffee, orange juice concentrate, and hot water in a saucepan, mixing well. Add the skim milk and the nonfat dry milk and heat until simmering. Remove from heat and add vanilla. Pour into small cups and garnish each with grated orange zest and dash of cinnamon.

Serves 4, demi-tasse servings

CHAPTER 12 **BASICS**

This chapter contains tips on ingredients and preparation techniques used throughout the book. It also includes recipes for ingredients called for in other recipes in this book. The inventive cook may enhance these basic recipes with personal variations. There is also a section on planning calcium-rich meals.

INGREDIENTS

Below is some helpful information on some of the ingredients used in the preceding recipes, as well as background on some calcium-rich substitutes.

Cheese

Cheese is a choice calcium food, a concentrated source of many of milk's nutrients. But attention must be paid to the cholesterol, fat, and sodium content of the many different varieties of cheese. There are choices to be made for taste and cooking method.

Cheese can be used in sandwiches, soups, salads, vegetables, sauces, casseroles, and dips; as a main dish; or with fruit for dessert. Cooking with cheese should be done quickly and at low temperatures, or by browning quickly under the broiler.

Read labels carefully for content when purchasing cheese, and store it, well wrapped, in the refrigerator. Some cheeses may be frozen. Imitation cheeses or cheese foods are made from vegetable oil and casein (milk protein), and, while they are low in cholesterol, their fat and calorie content remains high.

Low-fat cottage cheese (1%), part-skim ricotta cheese, and combinations with buttermilk, nonfat dry milk, yogurt, and skim milk play an important role in the high-calcium diet. Part-skim mozzarella cheese is also recommended because it melts well, imparts a nice flavor, and is lower in fat than many other cheeses. High-calcium, low-calorie recipes also call for small amounts of grated Parmesan or Romano and sapsago, a low-fat hard cheese with a sharp herbed flavor that is suitable for grating.

Cheddar cheese imparts a special flavor, but it is high in fat and calories, and a little can go a long distance.

The following chart will be helpful in making other cheese selections:

Cheese	Calories	Fat (g)	Calcium (mg)
LOW-FAT CHEESES			
Bon Bel, reduced-calorie, 1 oz. Mild, similar to Edam. Good for dessert or snacks.	60	4	209
Cheddar-style, 1 oz. Sharp flavor, good in sandwiches, casseroles, sauces. Some low-fat brands: Heidi Ann, Ryser, Tendale	70–83	4–5	200–260
Colby, Borden's Lite Line, 1 oz. Mild flavor for salads, sandwiches, snacks, casseroles.	50	2	200
Cottage Cheese, 4 oz. (½ cup): • Low-Fat 1% • Low-Fat 2% Mild taste, good for baking, dips, blends, sauces.	80 101	1 2	69 77
Farmer Cheese, May-bud, 1 oz. Clean flavor, good for baking, molds, dumplings, cooking.	90	2	150
Mozzarella, part-skim, 1 oz. Mild flavor, good for pizzas, melts, sauces, grilled vegetables, and baked casseroles.	72	5	—
Muenster, Borden's Lite Line, 1 oz. Semisoft, for snacks, melts, sandwiches.	50	2	200
Ricotta, part-skim, 1 oz. Semisweet flavor, good for cooked dishes, dips, combinations, fillings, desserts.	43	3	84
Swiss, 1 oz.: • Pasteurized Process Light 'n Lively, Kraft • Borden's Lite Line Mild, nutty sweet flavor, used for salads, sandwiches, fondue, casseroles.	71 50	4 2	214 200

Cheese	Calories	Fat (g)	Calcium (mg)
MODERATE-FAT CHEESES			
Edam, 1 oz. Mild, for appetizers, snacks, desserts with fruit.	101	8	207
Feta, 1 oz. White pickled cheese (sheep's or goat's milk), used in salads, soups, crumbled.	85	6	200
Goat's Milk Cheese, 1 oz. Good for dessert, salads, melts.	130	2	200
Parmesan, hard, 1 oz. Used grated in salads, breads, soups, sauces, vegetables, Italian dishes.	111	7	336
Romano, hard, 1 oz. Used grated in lieu of Parmesan.	110	8	302
Swiss, 1 oz. Mild, nutlike taste, used for snacks, sandwiches, fondue, dessert with fruit.	107	8	272
PASTEURIZED PROCESS CHEESE *PRODUCTS*			
Laughing Cow Reduced Calorie Wedges, 3/4 oz.	54	4.5	75
Kraft Light 'n Lively Singles, 1 oz.	77–84	6–7	143–161

Some cheese information used with permission of Dairy Nutrition Council Inc.

Formagg

A new product is currently hitting grocery markets nationwide. Formagg looks and tastes like real cheese, but it is made with polyunsaturated vegetable oil (instead of butter fat) and casein, a high-quality protein made from fresh milk. Formagg has 35 percent fewer calories than cheese, no cholesterol, and is loaded with vitamins and minerals. It is packaged shredded in plastic bags. Look for it in your grocer's cheese department, and use it as a replacement whenever natural cheese is required in baking, as a topping, and for melt dishes. It contains 30 mg calcium, 0 mg cholesterol, and 75 calories per 1-ounce serving.

Yogurt

Low-fat or nonfat plain yogurt is high in calcium. Yogurt is an acid food that helps to absorb iron and helps synthesize the B vitamins. It is more digestible than milk and is recommended for many people with lactose intolerance. It is an excellent source of protein and combines well with herbs, mustard, soy sauce, ginger, and sweeteners such as fructose, vanilla extract, fresh fruit, vegetables, and other skim milk products such as ricotta cheese, cottage cheese, and butter-milk. Draining yogurt (see Yogurt Sour Cream recipe on pg. 254) lets the whey escape and makes a solid, cheese yogurt that may be served plain or in recipes. Fresh batches of yogurt may be made as needed (see Your Own Yogurt recipe on pg. 254) by using a little yogurt mixed with milk.

Kefir

Kefir, which is now enjoying a renaissance on the American dairy scene, is delicious and may be used in place of plain yogurt, provided it is low-fat. Resembling sour cream in taste and texture, kefir may be acceptable for the lactose intolerant and provides about 85 calories and 160 mg of calcium per 8-ounce serving. Kefir cheese, another new product, contains 40 mg of calcium per 1-ounce serving.

Milk

The milk products called for in this cookbook are either nonfat, skim, or low-fat (1% fat, as in the case of cottage cheese).

- Buttermilk provides 99 calories per cup and 1% milk fat.
- Chocolate milk contains 179 calories per cup and 2% milk fat.
- 1% (low-fat) milk contains 102 calories per cup and 1% milk fat.
- 2% (low-fat) milk contains 121 calories per cup and 2% milk fat.
- Skim milk contains 86 calories per cup and less than 1% milk fat.
- Nonfat dry, instant, reconstituted milk contains 82 calories per cup and almost no fat.
- Evaporated skim milk contains 100 calories per cup and about 300 mg of calcium when diluted.
- Evaporated goat's milk contains 160 calories, 8 grams of fat, and 240 mg of calcium per 4-ounce serving, undiluted.
- Low-fat plain yogurt contains 144 calories per cup and 4 grams of fat.
- Nonfat yogurt contains 110 calories per cup and no fat.
- 1% (low-fat) cottage cheese contains 80 calories per cup and 1 gram of fat.

When shopping, purchase milk and milk products just before getting into the checkout line. Read the dates and refrigerate as soon as possible. Don't pour unused milk back into the container, but keep it refrigerated in a separate bowl. Keep dry milk tightly closed and store in a cool, dry place.

Goat's Milk and Its Cheese

Becoming increasingly important among the American cheeses, goat's milk cheese is an excellent calcium source and is lower in fat content than many other cheeses, with 40–50 percent of its calories coming from fat, compared to about 80 percent of calories coming from fat in regular cow's milk cheeses. Goat's milk and yogurt may also be tolerated better by those who can not tolerate cow's milk.

Miracle Evaporated Goat Milk is enriched with folic acid and Vitamin D, and a 4-ounce serving contains 30 percent calcium. Powdered goat's milk is also available.

Nonfat Dry Milk

An easy way to get a calcium boost is to add nonfat dry milk powder to recipes. It provides 50 milligrams of calcium per teaspoon. It can be added to chopped meats, soups, salad dressings, baked goods, drinks, and desserts. It disappears and is relatively tasteless. Buttermilk is also available in powdered form and is useful for baking and mixing blender beverages.

A Note on Lactose Intolerance

Lactose powder or Lactaid drops are available and can be added to milk to break down the lactose. Lactaid makes CalciMilk, which is available in many super-market dairy departments. It has 500 mg of calcium per 8-ounce serving. The person who suffers lactose intolerance may be able to digest goat's milk, kefir, yogurt, and acidophilus milk. Soy milk also provides calcium and may be tolerated more readily. Soy milk is now available in supermarkets, or it can be made at home (see recipe on pg. 252).

Miso

Miso has been used in Japanese cuisine for centuries and is a useful, calcium- and protein-laden paste made of fermented soybeans or barley. It can be purchased in health food stores and oriental markets. Use it in making dips and spreads, as a soup base, or in salad dressings. Miso is available in light and dark versions. It is low in fat and calories and considered by the Japanese to be a gift from the gods. Store in refrigerator.

Nuts

Almonds and filberts, also known as hazelnuts, have a goodly amount of calcium. But they also contain high fat. Use them sparingly to add crunch. Buy them raw in a reliable health food store and beware of any soft or dried nuts as those might be toxic. Roast before using.

Seaweed

Minerals abound in the sea. Hence a number of different seaweeds are valuable additional sources of calcium. The Japanese rely on many different kinds of seaweed for their iron, magnesium, and calcium. Health food stores and oriental markets are the best outlets. Here are some of the varieties to be found:

- *Hijiki*—Tastes a little like licorice. Very high in calcium. Use it in soup and salads.
- *Wakame*—A dark green leaf that needs to be soaked before using. Use in soups, on top of fish, in dressings.
- *Kombu*—A giant kelp plant that is found dried and shredded. Useful sprinkled over fish, chicken, rice, or vegetable dishes.
- *Nori*—Easy to toast as it comes in square sheets. Toast dried sheets of seaweed over stovetop burner or under broiler, then simply crumble over fish, salads, vegetables, pasta.
- *Dulse*—A red, Canadian seaweed used in cooking fish and stews.

None of these seaweeds has any calories to speak of, but they are chock-full of vitamins and minerals and also provide sodium.

Seaweed or kelp may be added to beans and legumes, soups, potatoes, rice, and other dishes.

Agar-agar also comes from the sea. It may be used in place of powdered gelatin. It is fairly costly and can be found in health food and oriental stores. It delivers a mighty punch of calcium.

All of the seaweed products listed above may be ordered from Katagiri, 224 E. 59th St., New York, NY 10022. Eden Foods (Clinton, MI 49236) also imports and distributes many of these products. Maine Coast Sea Vegetables (Franklin, ME 04634; (207) 565-2907) raises and packages a variety of American seaweeds.

Tofu

Tofu is available in health food stores, oriental markets, and many supermarkets. Use the kind made with calcium sulfate. Tofu made with calcium sulfate yields

139 milligrams of calcium per 3.5-ounce serving. Keep covered with water in the refrigerator and change water daily. Use diced in soup, mashed in casseroles, sliced and sautéed (see Tofu Sauté recipe on pg. 253), or broiled after marinating. Tofu has no taste of its own and takes on the flavor of its companion ingredients. Because it soaks up water, it is best to drain the tofu between paper towels and under a weight to draw out the excess moisture. Tofu may be used in place of croutons over vegetables. Combined with frozen bananas or other fruit, it makes a fine dessert and can also be used to make spreads and appetizers, sauces, drinks, and dressings. Firm tofu cakes are better for cooking. The silken or soft tofu is best used for drinks or dessert mixtures.

Ginger

Use fresh gingerroot whenever possible. Wash and grate without peeling. Store in bottle of sherry and refrigerate until ready to use.

Herbs

Herbs are the key to tastier dishes and sauces. Rosemary, tarragon, basil, oregano, dill, and many others can make the difference in fish dishes, dips, dressings, poultry recipes, and vegetables. If dried herbs are used rather than fresh, use about one-third of the fresh amount. To have a good year-round supply of basil on hand, gather the fresh basil leaves and place in blender or processor with a little water. Freeze in ice cube trays, then transfer to small storage containers and keep in freezer until ready to use.

SOME HOW-TO HINTS FOR PREPARATION

To Blanch

Vegetables retain their nutrients and crispness when cooked in boiling water for about 2 minutes and then refreshed quickly under cold water. They may then be served with dips or in salads with desired dressings. Nuts are also blanched in boiling water and the skins then rubbed away.

To Make Bread Crumbs

Place toasted or stale whole wheat bread in food processor and cut into chunks or finer, as desired. Store in tightly closed container in freezer until ready to use.

To Beat Egg Whites

Let egg whites stand at room temperature before beating. They will then whip more readily.

Freezing

Freeze summer berries and vegetables such as red or yellow bell peppers for use during the year. To freeze berries, do not wash, but pick them over and hull. Spread out on cookie sheet and place in freezer until solid. Transfer to baggies or freezer containers and store in freezer. Defrost before using. For the peppers, trim and slice into thin strips or dice them and freeze in the same manner.

To Make Ice Cream, Ices, and Sherbets

Ice cream machines are generally available, but if one is not on hand, there is an excellent method for making ices and sherbets. After mixing ingredients, pour into a shallow metal pan or metal ice tray. Cover and place in freezer until a band of ice appears around the edges. This may take 1–2 hours, depending on how efficient the freezer is. Break up the ice crystals by stirring briskly with a fork. Cover and return to freezer and repeat the beating and freezing procedure every 30 minutes or so. Just before serving, the mixture may be turned back into a food processor or into a bowl and beaten with an electric mixer. Serve when the mixture is slightly mushy after last beating or let it soften in refrigerator before dishing out.

To Julienne

To make thin julienne strips of bell peppers, citrus zest, carrots, celery, radishes, or other vegetables, trim away curved or spotted parts and cut into matchstick-shaped slices about 2 inches long, ¼ inch wide.

To Shuck Oysters

Always purchase fresh oysters from a reliable fish market. Scrub them thoroughly with a stiff brush under running water. Break off shells at the thin end. Hold an oyster in the palm of your hand with hinged end toward you. Force an oyster knife between shells at broken end and twist to force apart. Cut the large muscle, which is close to the flat upper shell. Break off and discard flat shell. Slide knife under the oyster meat to release it.

To Prepare Lobster

To cook lobsters, fill a large kettle or steamer with water to depth of 1 inch and bring to a boil. Place live lobsters in pot and cover. Steam for about 7 minutes, until lobster turns red, for lobsters weighing around a pound. For larger sizes, steam a bit longer. When cooked, lift lobsters out of pot and lightly push shells away from body to drain out excess fluid. Crack claws. Use a sharp knife to split lengthwise and remove the hard sand sac located between the eyes. All other parts of the lobster may be eaten.

To cut up a live lobster before cooking, drive the point of a sharp knife into the head on the underside of shell and force knife through to tail. This kills the lobster instantly and it may then be cut into smaller pieces.

To Prepare Nuts

Blanching Nuts

To blanch nuts, drop them into a pot of boiling water for a few minutes. Remove, drain, and rub off the skins. They are now ready to be sliced or chopped.

Roasting Nuts

To roast nuts, spread them on a baking pan, sprinkle with a little cinnamon if desired, and bake in preheated 350°F oven for about 15 minutes, until lightly browned. Store in tightly closed container.

To Toast Seeds

To toast sesame, sunflower, or pumpkin seeds, heat a nonstick skillet, add seeds, cover, and warm the seeds until they begin to pop. Shake the pan to keep them from burning. Remove and spread out on paper toweling to blot up any released oils. Store in a covered jar in refrigerator.

To Make Soup Stocks

Make large batches of your favorite recipe for vegetable, chicken, and beef broth and keep in the freezer in small, covered containers. When preparing a recipe that calls for stock, defrost ahead of time or heat in a saucepan. For small quantities, freeze the stock in ice cube trays and then store in baggies. When bones are used to make stock, be certain to add some plain vinegar, lemon juice, or tomatoes, as these acid ingredients draw out the calcium in the bones.

BASIC BEEF STOCK

4 pounds shin bones with meat

3 quarts water

1 cup sliced onions

1 cup sliced carrots

1 cup chopped celery

1 bay leaf

½ teaspoon dried thyme

8 whole peppercorns

4 sprigs fresh parsley

3 cloves

1 clove garlic

Cover shin bones with cold water in a large kettle and bring to a boil. Cook for two minutes and then drain. Return the bones to the kettle and add 3 quarts of water and the remaining ingredients. Return to boil and simmer for 4 hours, skimming off any fat and residue that accumulates. Strain stock and discard the solids. Refrigerate in a bowl and skim off any further fat. Then pour into individually measured containers and keep in freezer for future use.

Makes 10 cups

CHICKEN STOCK

1 fryer chicken or stewing hen, skin removed

4 tablespoons vinegar

4 cloves garlic, chopped

2 ribs celery with tops, chopped roughly

2 medium onions, chopped

1 carrot, scraped and trimmed

1 parsnip, scraped and trimmed

6 sprigs parsley

1 bay leaf

6 peppercorns

8 cups water

PER CUP:
Calcium (mg): 39
Fat (g): 1.3
Chol (mg): 22
Carbo (g): 11
Protein (g): 9.6
Calories (g): 94

Bring all ingredients to a boil in a large kettle. Cook uncovered over low heat for 15 minutes, removing any residue that accumulates. Reduce heat and simmer for 2 to 3 hours. Remove cover and let cool. Strain, pressing meat to draw out liquid. Save chicken pieces for use in enchiladas, salads, or other dishes. Discard other solids. Refrigerate in a bowl and skim off any further fat. Stock should be used within a few days or frozen in small containers for future use.

Makes 6 cups

VEGETABLE STOCK

Two methods are equally good for preparing a rich base for soup and sauce. The first is simply collecting the water left from cooking various vegetables. Blend together and store in refrigerator until ready to use. The second method is to use a kind of compost collection of all your vegetable parings and unused tops and excess vegetable pieces. Collect in a plastic bag. After a day or two add water or vegetable juices, place in saucepan, bring to a boil, and simmer for about 30 minutes. Then strain, place in small containers (or in an ice cube tray), and freeze until ready to use. (No nutrient figures are given since the amounts are negligible.)

BASIC BROWN RICE

PER 1/2-CUP
SERVING:
Calcium (mg): 117
Fat (g): 3
Chol (mg): 1
Carbo (g): 1
Protein (g): 2.4
Calories (g): 117

1 cup brown rice, rinsed well until water runs clear

2 cups water or Vegetable Stock (see pg. 247)

Place rice in 2 cups of boiling liquid and cover. Simmer for 30 minutes over low heat without stirring, but checking to make certain there is enough liquid left. Remove from heat and let steam, covered, for another 10 minutes. Season, fluff, and serve.

Vegetables such as peas, mushrooms, celery, onions, carrots, or scallions may be added, as well as any additional seasoning such as soy sauce or curry. These may be added before the steaming or stirred in later.

Note: The basic rule of thumb is two parts water to one part rice. To hasten cooking, soak rice for an hour or so before cooking. Rice may also be cooked in skim milk for added calcium. Cooked rice can be used to make pie crust. Spread 1 cup rice in pie tin, pat down, and bake in preheated 350°F oven for 10 minutes.

Makes 3 cups

BASIC WHITE SAUCE

> 1 tablespoon Best Butter (recipe below)
>
> 1 tablespoon arrowroot
>
> 1 cup evaporated skim milk
>
> ⅛ teaspoon salt
>
> ⅛ teaspoon white pepper

PER TABLESPOON
BASIC WHITE
SAUCE:
Calcium (mg): 19
Fat (g): .8
Chol (mg): 1
Carbo (g): 1.8
Protein (g): 1.1
Calories (g): 23

Heat Best Butter in nonstick skillet, then stir in arrowroot. Gradually add milk, stirring until sauce thickens. Season with salt and pepper. For thicker sauce, add more butter and more arrowroot.

PER TABLESPOON
CHEESE SAUCE:
Calcium (mg): 28
Fat (g): 1.2
Chol (mg): 3
Carbo (g): 1.9
Protein (g): 1.4
Calories (g): 25

Variations:

Cheese Sauce (Mornay): Add ¼ cup cubed Cheddar, Parmesan, grated low-fat cheese, or Formagg and stir into the white sauce to melt.

Mushroom Cream Sauce: Add 6 chopped mushrooms and 1 chopped sautéed scallion to white sauce. Blend well and simmer for 5 minutes.

PER TABLESPOON
MUSHROOM
SAUCE:
Calcium (mg): 29
Fat (g): .7
Chol (mg): 1
Carbo (g): 1.5
Protein (g): 1.5
Calories (g): 34

Makes 1 cup or 16 tablespoons

BEST BUTTER

> 1 cup polyunsaturated oil such as safflower, sunflower seed, corn, vegetable, soybean, walnut, vegetable, or combination
>
> 1 cup whipped butter
>
> ½ teaspoon salt

PER TABLESPOON:
Calcium (mg): 1
Fat (g): 11.1
Chol (mg): 11.6
Carbo (g): 0
Protein (g): .1
Calories (g): 98

Mix ingredients together in blender or food processor. Store in refrigerator or freezer. May be herbed with garlic, scallions, mustard, tarragon, dill, etc. It is best when stored in the freezer.

Makes 2 cups or 32 tablespoons

CRÈME FRAÎCHE

PER SERVING:
Calcium (mg): 46
Fat (g): 1.3
Chol (mg): 5
Carbo (g): 1
Protein (g): 1.9
Calories (g): 23

1 cup part-skim ricotta cheese

¼ cup buttermilk

Whip both ingredients in a blender until smooth. Heat in a small nonstick saucepan until just warm. Pour into a small jar and let stand for 8 hours at room temperature. Stir, cover, and chill until serving.

Makes 1 cup or 16, 1-tablespoon servings

GRAHAM CRACKER CRUST

PER SERVING
(CRUST ONLY):
Calcium (mg): 3
Fat (g): 4.1
Chol (mg): 0
Carbo (g): 51
Protein (g): .6
Calories (g): 57

2 tablespoons walnut oil

1 cup graham cracker crumbs (place crackers in food processor or blender to crumble)

Add walnut oil to the crumbs in blender or processor and blend well. Pat down in an 8-inch pie plate. Bake 10 minutes in pre-heated 350°F oven. Remove and let cool before filling. May be used with Carob Cream, Lime Filling, Peanut Ricotta Sauce, or Mocha Filling (see pgs. 222–225 for pie recipes). Also good lined with fruit and topped with yogurt, ricotta, or cottage cheese blends.

Makes 1 crust for a pie to serve 8

GREAT GRAPE JELLY

PER SERVING:
Calcium (mg): 1
Fat (g): 0
Chol (mg): 0
Carbo (g): 38
Protein (g): .1
Calories (g): 16

1 cup unsweetened grape juice

3 tablespoons instant or granulated tapioca

Pour grape juice into saucepan and add tapioca. Let stand 10 minutes. Then bring to a boil over medium heat and stir. Remove from heat and let cool. Pour into a jar and keep refrigerated.

Makes 1 cup or 16, 1-tablespoon servings

LOW-FAT CREAM CHEESE

1 tablespoon nonfat dry milk

4 tablespoons Best Butter (see pg. 249)

2 tablespoons safflower oil

1 cup low-fat cottage cheese

PER SERVING:
Calcium (mg): 12
Fat (g): 3
Chol (mg): 4
Carbo (g): .5
Protein (g): 1.8
Calories (g): 37

Blend all ingredients together and refrigerate, covered.

Variation: Flavor with chives, scallions, or as desired.

Makes 1 cup or 16, 1-tablespoon servings

MAKE-BELIEVE MAYO

1 cup low-fat cottage cheese

2 tablespoons safflower oil

1 tablespoon apple cider vinegar

$\frac{1}{2}$ teaspoon salt

Dash white pepper

PER SERVING:
Calcium (mg): 9
Fat (g): 1.8
Chol (mg): 1
Carbo (g): .4
Protein (g): 1.8
Calories (g): 25

Blend all ingredients until smooth. Refrigerate, covered, for at least 24 hours before using.

Variation: May be mixed with tomato paste, mustard, pickles, or any herbs as desired.

Makes 1 cup or 16, 1-tablespoon servings

PERFECT PIE CRUST

PER SERVING
(CRUST ONLY):
Calcium (mg): 12
Fat (g): 7.1
Chol (mg): 0
Carbo (g): 14.7
Protein (g): 3.1
Calories (g): 133

½ cup whole wheat flour

½ cup all-purpose unbleached flour

¼ teaspoon salt

3 tablespoons safflower oil

3 tablespoons ice water (or more if needed)

2 tablespoons buttermilk

1 egg white

Sift the flours and salt together into a mixing bowl, then stir in the oil, ice water, and buttermilk. Knead dough 3 or 4 times until it is moist and elastic. Roll into a ball, cover, and refrigerate 15 minutes. Place between 2 sheets of wax paper and roll dough into a 12-inch circle. Place in a 9-inch pie tin. Trim edges and finish by pressing with a fork or pastry knife. If baking the shell empty, prick a few holes in the dough. Brush shell with egg white and refrigerate for 10 minutes. Bake in preheated 350°F oven for 10 minutes, until brown. The same dough may be used to make tart shells, using an inverted cup to cut the dough and baking the crust in muffin tins.

Makes 1 crust for a pie to serve 8 or 8 tart shells

SOY MILK

PER 1-CUP
SERVING:
Calcium (mg): 95
Fat (g): 4.6
Chol (mg): 0
Carbo (g): 12.6
Protein (g): 15.6
Calories (g): 150

1 pound soy flour

3 quarts cold water

1 teaspoon pure vanilla extract

½ teaspoon salt

1 tablespoon crystalline fructose

Place flour and water in large saucepan and beat with a wire whisk until smooth. Cook over low heat, stirring, for about 20 minutes. Strain into a large bowl through cheesecloth-lined sieve. Mix in vanilla, salt, and fructose. Store, covered, in refrigerator.

Makes 3 quarts

TOFU SAUTÉ

1 tablespoon low-sodium soy sauce

1 teaspoon walnut or safflower oil

1 drop sesame oil

1 cake (about 1 cup) firm tofu (bean curd), sliced into ½-inch pieces

PER SERVING:
Calcium (mg): 155
Fat (g): 7.3
Chol (mg): 0
Carbo (g): 3.7
Protein (g): 10.2
Calories (g): 112

Mix soy sauce and oils together. Press tofu slices between paper towels and place heavy weight on top for 15 minutes. When drained of excess moisture, place in marinade and turn to coat all pieces. Sauté in nonstick skillet until brown on both sides. Broil if preferred. This is a basic method for cooking tofu, which may then be used in salads, as garnish, in stir-fried vegetables, in casseroles, or just nibbled as is.

Serves 2

WHIPPED RICOTTA CREAM

¾ cup low-fat cottage cheese

⅓ cup part-skim ricotta cheese

PER SERVING:
Calcium (mg): 19
Fat (g): .5
Chol (mg): 1.9
Carbo (g): .5
Protein (g): 1.8
Calories (g): 14

Place cottage cheese in a small strainer and quickly rinse under cold water. Squeeze out any excess moisture. Place drained cottage cheese and ricotta in blender and whip until smooth. This is lovely as a topping combined with sugarless fruit conserve such as raspberry, apricot, or peach (use 2 teaspoons per cup of cheese).

Makes 1 cup or 16, 1-tablespoon servings

YOGURT SOUR CREAM

PER SERVING:
Calcium (mg): 26
Fat (g): .2
Chol (mg): 1
Carbo (g): 1
Protein (g): .7
Calories (g): 9

PER SERVING
OF VARIATION:
Calcium (mg): 27
Fat (g): .2
Chol (mg): 1
Carbo (g): 1.8
Protein (g): .8
Calories (g): 13

Herbs (optional)
16 ounces plain low-fat or nonfat yogurt

If desired, mix herbs such as dill, tarragon, parsley, or caraway seed into the yogurt. Place yogurt in a cheesecloth-lined sieve and let it drip over a bowl in refrigerator for 4–6 hours or overnight, until the yogurt has the consistency of sour cream. The whey that drips out may be reserved for use in making soups or breads.

Variation: To make orange-flavored Yogurt Sour Cream, use 2 tablespoons concentrated frozen orange juice and a little cinnamon instead of the herbs for a sweet sauce.

Makes 1 cup or 16, 1-tablespoon servings

YOUR OWN YOGURT

PER CUP:
Calcium (mg): 411
Fat (g): .6
Chol (mg): 6
Carbo (g): 16.2
Protein (g): 11.4
Calories (g): 118

1 quart skim milk or goat's milk
1 tablespoon plain low-fat yogurt

Pour milk into a saucepan and bring to a boil. Let cool to body temperature. Put the yogurt into a wide-mouthed jar and pour the milk over it, whisking. Cover and place in a warm spot for about 8 hours. Chill before using. Some of this yogurt may be used for future batches, but use the commercial yogurt as starter every so often.

Makes about 3 cups

PLANNING CALCIUM-RICH MEALS

Plan meals so that there is a balance from the four essential food groups: milk, grains, fruit, and vegetables. Know the number of calories you need for each meal during the day, noting the total calories needed at different times of the day. The nutritional data that appear with each recipe indicate the amount of calcium, protein, carbohydrate, fat, cholesterol, and calories it contains. Add up the numbers of all the dishes you select to get your total daily intake. After a while this will become second nature.

You may wish to make a meal of a soup, salad, and bread. Or you may prefer an appetizer, entree, vegetable, and dessert. In planning nutritionally balanced meals, keep in mind the following recommended percentages of the food groups:

Protein	10–20 percent
Carbohydrates	50–60 percent
Fat	20–25 percent, with no more than 10 percent saturated
Cholesterol	no more than 200 milligrams daily or 100 milligrams cholesterol per 1,000 calories
Fiber	25 grams per 1,000 calories

Vary your food choices so that there are good balances of whole grains and seeds, fish, milk, and fresh vegetables.

Be aware of the following:
- Too much protein inhibits the effectiveness of calcium.
- Smoking and drinking alcohol may put you at greater risk of osteoporosis.
- Coffee is now known to prevent calcium absorption and its use should therefore be limited. Stress increases your need for calcium. Some medicines, such as cortisone, antacids, and laxatives, may interfere with the absorption of calcium.
- Weight-bearing exercise on a regular basis helps to keep bones healthy.
- Young women should not exercise excessively since this may cause amenorrhea which depletes calcium. Exposure to sunshine and vitamin D-fortified milk products are essential to good bone growth.
- High fiber intake may interfere with calcium absorption.

Average calcium requirements:

- Children need 1,000 milligrams of calcium a day.
- Teenagers require 1,000 milligrams of calcium a day. Pregnant and nursing women require at least 1,500 milligrams a day.
- Pregnant and nursing teenagers need 1,600 or more milligrams daily.
- Adult women require 1,000 milligrams daily up to menopause and 1,500 milligrams thereafter, unless estrogen is prescribed.
- Adult men require 1,500 milligrams daily.

APPENDIX

CALCIUM-RICH FOODS

DAIRY GROUP	**Milligrams of Calcium**
Milk, 1 cup	
Buttermilk	285
1% low-fat	300
2% low-fat	297
Skim (fat-free)	302
Evaporated skim milk, undiluted	738
Nonfat dry milk, unreconstituted	1,508
Goat's milk, 1 cup	326
Yogurt, 1 cup	
Plain low-fat	415
Plain skim milk	452

SEAFOOD/BEANS GROUP	**Milligrams of Calcium**
Beans, dried, cooked, 1 cup	90
Oysters, raw, 7–9	113
Salmon, canned, with bones, 3 ounces	167
Sardines, canned, with bones, 3 ounces	372
Shrimp, canned, 3 ounces	99

VEGETABLE GROUP	**Milligrams of Calcium**
½ cup, cooked, from fresh	
Beet greens	72
Bok choy	126
Broccoli	68
Collards	179
Dandelion greens	147
Kale	103
Mustard greens	97
Spinach	84
Tofu, processed with calcium sulfate, 4 ounces	145
Turnip greens	267

GRAIN GROUP

	Milligrams of Calcium
Soy flour, $\frac{1}{2}$ cup	132
Waffle, 7-inch diameter	179
Pancakes, 4-inch diameter, serving of 2	116
Cornbread, 2 x 2 inches	94

NUTS AND SEEDS ($\frac{1}{2}$ cup)

	Milligrams of Calcium
Almonds	166
Brazil nuts	130
Hazelnuts	141
Pistachios	86
Sesame seeds	83
Pumpkin seeds	87

OTHER

	Milligrams of Calcium
Blackstrap molasses, 1 tablespoon	137
Dried figs, 10	269
Miso, 1 tablespoon	150

Agar-Agar and the following seaweeds are notably endowed with calcium: Dulse, Hijiki, Kombu, Wakame

INDEX

A

Almond
Apple Ice Cream, 198
Carob Milk Shake, 228
Delight, 210
Ginger Sauce, 162
Rice Pilaf, 132
Anchovy Yogurt Dressing, 162
Appetizers, 1–22
Apple Pancakes, 91
Apricot Mousse, 212
Artichokes, 105
Asparagus and Pimiento, 105
Asparagus Potage, 24
Avocado Dressing, Creamy, 165
Avocado Smoothie, 2

B

Banana
Berry Rice Pudding, 213
Maple Ice Cream, 199
-Pineapple Shake, 233
Shake, 230
Sweet Potato Pudding, 214
Tofu Ice Cream, 200
Barley and Mushroom Soup, 38
Bean(s)
Black, and Salmon Dip, 3
Green, Amandine, 112
Green, Dilled, 111
Salad, Mexicali, 148
Soup, 26, 36
Beef Casserole, Green Noodle and, 49
Beef Stock, 246
Berries and Yogurt à l'Orange, 216
Beverages, 227–236
Bisque, Lobster and Tomato, 33
Bisque, Salmon, 40

blanching, 243
Blintzes and Fillings, 93, 95
Blue Cheese Dressing, 163
Blueberry Buttermilk Bake, 98
Bluefish Dulse, Baked, 60
Bok Choy, 106
Borscht, Pink, 35
bread crumbs, how to make, 243
Bread Pudding, Carob-Nut, 184
Breads, 181–191
Broccoli
Buttermilk Soup, 25
and Cauliflower Bake, 107
Ricotta Pie, 87
Sesame, 106
Brown Bread, Boston, 182
Brussels Sprouts, Onion-Creamed, 108
Bulgur and Vegetable Cream, 130
Burgers, Goat's Cheese, 48
Butter, Best, 249
Buttermilk
Blueberry Bake, 98
Broccoli Soup, 25
Cucumber Soup, 31
Mustard Dressing, 164
Soda Bread, 183

C

Cabbage Bread, Green and Red, 187
Cabbage, Spicy Yogurt, 109
Cabbage and Sprouts, 109
calcium
foods rich in, 257, 258
importance of in diet, iv–vii, ix
in meal planning, 255
requirements in diet, 256
Cannellini Soup, 27

Cantaloupe Sherbet, 206
Carioca Bean Soup, 26
Carob
Almond Milk Shake, 228
Cream, 211
Cream Pie, 222
-Nut Bread Pudding, 184
Carrot Salad, 143
Carrot Soup, 30
Casserole, Green Noodle and Beef, 49
Casserole, Macaroni, Tomato, and Cheese, 83
Cauliflower and Broccoli Bake, 107
Caviar Cheese Dip, 4
Cheddar Bread, 191
Cheese
Blue Dandelion Salad, 146
Blue, Dressing, 163
and Caviar Dip, 4
and Chicken Salad, 144
Clam Dip, 5
Goat's, Salad, 145
information on, 237
Liptauer, 10
and Mango Sauce, 175
[Mozzarella] Melt, 151
Sauce, 249
and Tofu Soufflé, 100
and Tomato Broil, 123
Tomato, and Macaroni Casserole, 83
Tortellini in Cheese Sauce, 84
Chicken
and Cheese Salad, 144
Curry, Murgi, 55
à la King, 53
Rollups, Mozzarella, 54
Spinach Bake, 57
Stock, 247
with Yogurt, 56

Chiffon, Orange, 178
Chili-Cheese Cornbread, 185
Chili con Queso, 4
Chocolate, Hot, Cinnamon, 235
Chowder, Corn, Mexican, 37
Chowder, Shrimp, 41
Clam Cheese Dip, 5
Coleslaw, Red and Green, 153
Collards, Hot, 110
Coquilles St. Jacques, 70
Corn Chowder, Mexican, 37
Cornbread, Chili-Cheese, 185
Cornmeal Muffins, 193
Cottage Cheese Soufflé, 101
Cottage Cheese Soup, 28
Cottage Cheese and Vegetable Salad, 157
Crab Gratin, 62
Cream Cheese, Low-Fat, 251
Cream, Whipped Ricotta, 253
Crème Fraîche, 250
Crust, Graham Cracker, 250
Crust, Perfect Pie, 252
Cucumber Buttermilk Soup, 31
Cucumber Salad, Middle Eastern, 150
Curry, Murgi Chicken, 55
Curry Sauce, 174
Curry Shrimp and Scallops, 73
Custard Cups, Coffee, 208
Custard, Peanut, 209

D
Dandelion Blue Cheese Salad, 146
Desserts, 197–227
Dips and Spreads, 2–15, 168
Dressings, Salad, 161–172

E
Eggnog, 228
Egg Watercress Salad, 159
Entrees, 47–102

F
Farofa, Brazilian, 128
Fennel Dip, 7
Figs, Stuffed, 220
Fish Bake, Indian, 61

Fish Rolls, Green and White, 74
Formagg, 239
Frappe, Fran's, 229
freezing, how to, 244
French Toast, 96
Frittata, Tofu, 89
Fruit Delight, 221
Fruit Desserts, 216–221
Fruit Sauce, Yogurt, 179
Fudge Freeze, 201

G
Garbanzo Salad, 147
Garlic Dressing, Creamy, 166
Ginger Bread, Orange, 189
ginger, information on, 243
Graham Cracker Crust, 250
Grains, 127–132
Grape Jelly, 250
Grape Leaves, Stuffed, 22
Grape Sherbet, 207
Green Beans Amandine, 112
Green Beans, Dilled, 111
Green Goddess Soup, 34
Greens and Sardines, 154
Groats, Buckwheat, and Vegetables, 129
Guacamole, Vegetable, 8

H
herbs, information on, 243
Hors d'oeuvres, 16–22
Horseradish Dressing-Spread, 168
Hummus, 9

I
Ice Cream
    Almond Apple, 198
    Banana Maple, 199
    Banana Tofu, 200
    how to make, 244
    ingredients, information on, 237–243

J
Jelly, Grape, 250
julienne, how to, 244

K
Kale, Braised, 113
Kale and Potatoes, 135
Kale Soup, 32
Kebabs, Lamb, in Spinach Sauce, 50
kefir, 240
Kiwi Lime Pie, 223
Kohlrabi, Hungarian, 113

L
lactose intolerance, 241
Lamb Kebabs in Spinach Sauce, 50
Lasagna Rollups, Florentine, 79
Leek Potato Pie, 137
Leeks Vinaigrette, 114
Lemon Sauce, 174
Lime Kiwi Pie, 223
Lime and Yogurt Sauce, 175
Liptauer Cheese, 10
lobster, how to prepare, 244
Lobster Newburg, 63
Lobster and Tomato Bisque, 33

M
Macaroni, Tomato, and Cheese Casserole, 83
Mango Cheese Sauce, 175
Mango Mousse, 212
Manicotti, Mushroom, 81
Mayonnaise, Make-Believe, 251
"Mayonnaise," Yogurt, Fines Herbes, 172
meal planning, 255
measures and weights, 259
Melon, Mediterranean, 217
Melon Mixer, 231
milk, information on, 240
Milk Shake
    Carob Almond, 228
    Frozen Banana, 230
    Happy Health, 230
    Mocha, 231
    Pineapple-Banana, 233
    Tofu, 234
Milk, Soy, 252
Miso, 11
miso, information on, 241
Mixed Salad, Mexican, 149
Mocha Filling, 224

Mocha Milk Shake, 231
Mocha Sherbet, 207
Mornay Sauce, 249
Moussaka, Meatless, 88
Mousse, Apricot, 212
Mousse, Mango, 212
Mousse, Salmon Confetti, 65
Muffins, 192–196
Mushroom(s)
  and Barley Soup, 38
  Cream Sauce, 249
  Cream of, Soup, 29
  Manicotti, 81
  and Polenta, 131
  Sardine-Stuffed, 21
  and Spinach, Creamed, 119
Mustard Buttermilk Dressing,
  164

N
Noodle Pudding, Russian, 133
Noodles, Green, and Beef
  Casserole, 49
Noodles, Soba, Tofu Bake, 80
Nut(s)
  Bread, Norwegian, 188
  how to prepare, 245
  information on, 242
  and Spinach Salad, 156

O
Oat Bran Muffins, 194
Oat Bread, Cottage, 186
Oatmeal Soufflé, 99
Okra, 115
  Lady Rainbow, 114
  Pods, Marinated, 115
  Provençal, 116
Orange
  Bracer, 232
  Chiffon, 178
  Ginger Bread, 189
  Mist, 202
  and Spinach Salad, 156
osteoporosis, iv–vii
Oysters
  on the Half-Shell, 19
  how to shuck, 244
  and Scallop Salad, 72
  Stew, Quick, 64

P
Pancakes, Apple, 91
Pancakes, Puffy, 92
Papaya Pistachio Cream, 203
Papaya Puree, 176
Parfait, Raspberry, 218
Parmesan Gourmet Muffins,
  192
Parmesan Popovers, 195
Parsnip Puree, 117
Pasta, 79–84
Peach Freeze, 204
Peach Melba, 217
Peachy Slim Nog, 232
Peanut Butter, Ricotta, 178
Peas, Green, Paris, 117
Peppers, Bell
  Dressing, 169
  Pickle Spread
  Salad, 142
  and Squash Salad, 120
Pesto, Popeye, 177
Pickle Pepper Spread, 13
Pie, Carob Cream, 222
Pie Crust, Perfect, 252
Pie, Kiwi Lime, 223
Pilaf, Almond Rice, 132
Pimiento and Asparagus, 105
Pineapple-Banana Shake, 233
Pineapple Ginger Frogurt, 205
Pizza, Basic Crust, 76
Pizza Topping
  Mozzarella, Tomato, and
    Sardine, 78
  Ratatouille, 77
  Shrimp and Leek, 78
Polenta and Mushrooms, 131
Popovers, Parmesan, 195
Poppy Seed Sauce, 177
Potato(es)
  Gratin, Creamed, 134
  and Kale, 135
  Leek Pie, 137
  New, Salad, 136
  Sardine Salad, 152
  Stuffed, 138
  Torte, Swiss, 139
  Yam Treat, 140
  preparation, how-to hints, 243
Pudding
  Banana Berry Rice, 213

Banana Sweet Potato, 214
Bread, Carob-Nut, 184
Coffee Cream, 215

R
Raisin Ricotta Tarts, 225
Raspberry Parfait, 218
Rhubarb, Russian, 220
Rice
  Almond Pilaf, 132
  Brown, 248
  Pie, 86
  Pudding, Banana Berry, 213
Ricotta Broccoli Pie, 87
Ricotta Veal Loaf, 51
Rollups, Lasagna, Florentine,
  79
Russian Dressing, 170
Rutabaga Puree, 118

S
Salad Dressings, 161–172
Salad, Potato, 136
Salad, Squash and Peppers,
  120
Salads, 141–160
Salmon
  Bisque, 40
  and Black Bean Dip, 3
  Croquettes, 67
  Dip, 13
  Loaf Evelyn, 68
  Mousse, Confetti, 65
  Poached, with Horseradish
    Sauce, 66
  -Stuffed Peppers, 69
Salsa, Summer, 126
Sardine(s)
  Appetizer, Parmesan, 12
  and Greens, 154
  Potato Salad, 152
  Salad, Simple, 155
  Squash, 20
  -Stuffed Mushrooms, 21
Sauce, White, 248
Sauces, 173–180, 249
Scallop(s)
  [Coquilles St. Jacques], 70
  Delight, Red and Green, 71
  and Oyster Salad, 72
  and Shrimp, Curried, 73

Seafood, 60–75
seaweed, information on, 242
seeds, how to toast, 245
Sesame Bread, 190
Sherbet, Cantaloupe, 206
Sherbet, Grape, 207
Sherbet, Mocha, 207
Shrimp Chowder, 41
Shrimp and Scallops, Curried, 73
Snow Pea Salad, 155
Snow Pea Soup, Oriental, 39
Soda Bread, Buttermilk, 183
Sole Florentine, 75
Soufflé, Cheese and Tofu, 100
Soufflé, Cottage Cheese, 101
Soufflé, Oatmeal, 99
soup stock, how to make, 245
Soup Stock, 246, 247
Soups, 23–46
Sour Cream, Yogurt, 254
Soy Milk, 252
Spinach, 120 ·
  Appetizer, 14
  Chicken Bake, 57
  and Mushrooms, Creamed, 119
  and Nut Salad, 156
  and Orange Salad, 156
Spreads, 2–15, 168
Squash
  and Peppers Salad, 120
  Sardine, 20
  Soup, 42
  Yogurt-Stuffed, 121
Stew, Oyster, 64
Stew, Vegetable Veal, 52
Stir-Fry, Vegetable Medley, 125
Stock, Soup, 246, 247
stock, soup, how to make, 245

Strawberry Freeze, 229
Stroganoff, Turkey, 59
Summer [vegetable] Soup, 43
supplements, dietary, v, vi, ix
Swiss Chard, 122

T
Tamale Pie, 85
Tarts, Ricotta Raisin, 225
Tofu
  and Cheese Soufflé, 100
  Dressing, Creamy, 167
  Frittata, 89
  information on, 242
  Parmesan, 90
  Sauté, 253
  Shake, 234
  Soba Noodle Bake, 80
  Sticks, 18
Tomato
  and Cheese Broil, 123
  Dip, 15
  and Lobster Bisque, 33
  Shake, 234
  Shorba, 44
  Velouté, 170
Tortellini in Cheese Sauce, 84
Turkey Divan, 58
Turkey Stroganoff, 59

V
Veal Loaf, Ricotta, 51
Veal Stew, Vegetable, 52
Vegetable(s), 103–126
  and Buckwheat Groats, 129
  Cottage Cheese Salad, 157
  Cream and Bulgur, 130
  Creamed, 124
  Dip, 6
  Guacamole, 8

Medley Stir-Fry, 125
Salad Bowl, 158
Stock, 247
Veal Stew, 52
Velouté, Tomato, 170
Vichyssoise, 45
Vienna Cream Sauce, 179
Vinaigrette, Balsamic, 163

W
Waffles, 97
Watercress Dressing, 171
Watercress Egg Salad, 159
weights and measures, 259
Whipped Cream, Ricotta, 253
White Sauce, 249

Y
Yam Potato Treat, 140
Yogurt
  Anchovy Dressing, 162
  and Berries à l'Orange, 216
  Cabbage, Spicy, 109
  with Chicken, 56
  Fruit Sauce, 179
  information on, 240
  and Lime Sauce, 175
  Loaf, 16
  "Mayonnaise" Fines Herbes, 172
  Soup, Turkish, 44
  Sour Cream, 254
  -Stuffed Squash, 121
  Your Own, 254

Z
Zucchini Salad, 159
Zucchini Soup, 46